SCHAUM'S *Easy* OUTLINES

PRINCIPLES OF
ECONOMICS

D1110809

Other Books in Schaum's Easy Outlines Series Include:

SCHAUM'S *Easy* OUTLINES

PRINCIPLES OF ECONOMICS

BASED ON SCHAUM'S
*Outline of Theory and Problems of
Principles of Economics (Second Edition)*
BY DOMINICK SALVATORE, Ph.D.
and
EUGENE A. DIULIO, Ph.D.

ABRIDGEMENT EDITOR
Wm. ALAN BARTLEY, Ph.D.

SCHAUM'S OUTLINE SERIES
McGRAW-HILL

*New York   Chicago   San Francisco   Lisbon   London   Madrid
Mexico City   Milan   New Delhi   San Juan
Seoul   Singapore   Sydney   Toronto*

The **McGraw·Hill** Companies

DOMINICK SALVATORE received his Ph.D. in 1971 and is currently Professor of Economics at Fordham University in New York. He is the author of several textbooks on economics and his research has been published in leading scholarly journals and presented at national and international conferences. He is the author of Schaum's Outlines of *Microeconomic Theory*, *Managerial Economics*, *Statistics and Econometrics*, and *International Economics*. He is also co-author of *Schaum's Outline of Developmental Economics*.

EUGENE A. DIULIO is Associate Professor of Economics at Fordham University and received his Ph.D. from Columbia University. He is the author of *Schaum's Outline of Macroeconomic Theory* and is an educational consultant to several banks. He also serves as an Adjunct Professor at the Columbia University Graduate School of Business.

WM. ALAN BARTLEY teaches Economics at Transylvania University in Lexington, Kentucky, where he received his B.A. in Economics and Finance. He received both an M.A. and Ph.D. degrees in Economics from Vanderbilt University. He is the author or co-author of articles published in professional journals, and he has presented several papers at professional meetings.

6 7 8 9 DOC DOC 0 9 8 7

ISBN 0-07-139873-2

Contents

Chapter 1
INTRODUCTION TO ECONOMICS

Methodology of Economics

Economics is a social science that studies individuals and organizations engaged in the production, distribution, and consumption of goods and services. The goal is to predict economic occurrences and to develop policies that might prevent or correct such problems as unemployment, inflation, or waste in the economy.

Economics is subdivided into macroeconomics and microeconomics. Macroeconomics studies aggregate output, employment, and the general price level. Microeconomics studies the economic behavior of individual decision makers such as consumers, resource owners, and business firms.

The discipline of economics has developed principles, theories, and models that isolate the most important determinants of economic events. In constructing a model, economists make assumptions to eliminate unnecessary detail to reduce the complexity of economic behavior. Once modeled, economic behavior may be presented as a relationship between dependent and independent variables. The behavior being explained is the dependent variable; the economic events explaining that behavior are the independent variables. The dependent variable may be presented as depending upon one independent variable, with the influence of the other independent variables held constant (the *ceteris paribus* assumption). An economic model will also specify whether the dependent and independent variables are positively or negatively related, i.e., moving in the same or opposite directions.

Note!

Ceteris paribus is Latin for "other things being equal." This phrase is used often by economists in modeling to isolate the relationship between specific dependent and independent variables.

Example 1.1

We shall assume that the amount a consumer spends (C) is positively related to her disposable income (Y_d), i.e., $C = f(Y_d)$. Table 1.1 presents data on consumer spending for five individuals with different levels of income. As seen in the table, consumption and disposable income display a positive relationship.

The data from Table 1.1 are plotted in Figure 1-1 and labeled C_1. The dependent variable, consumer spending, is plotted on the vertical axis and the independent variable, disposable income, is plotted on the horizontal axis. Graphs are used to present data and the positive or negative relationship of the dependent and independent variables visually.

Table 1.1
(in $)

Individual	Disposable Income (Y_d)	Consumption (C)
A	20,000	20,000
B	21,000	20,750
C	22,000	21,500
D	24,000	23,000
E	27,000	25,250

Problem of Scarcity

Economics is the study of scarcity—the study of the allocation of scarce resources to satisfy human wants. People's material wants, for the most part, are unlimited. Output, on the other hand, is limited by the state of

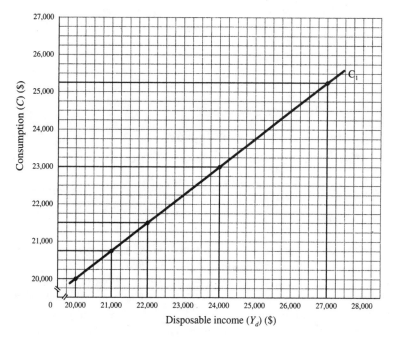

Figure 1-1

technology and the quantity and quality of the economy's resources. Thus, the production of each good and service involves a cost. A good is usually defined as a physical item such as a car or a hamburger, and a service is something provided to you such as insurance or a haircut.

Scarcity is a fundamental problem for every society. Decisions must be made regarding *what* to produce, *how* to produce it, and *for whom* to produce. *What* to produce involves decisions about the kinds and quantities of goods and services to produce. *How* to produce requires decisions about what techniques to use and how economic resources (or factors of production) are to be combined in producing output. The economic resources used to produce goods and services include:

- **Land**. The economy's natural resources—such as land, trees, and minerals.
- **Labor**. The mental and physical skills of individuals in a society.
- **Capital**. Goods—such as tools, machines, and factories—used in production or to facilitate production.

The *for whom* to produce involves decisions on the distribution of output among members of a society.

Remember

Economics helps to solve the three important questions of *what* to produce, *how* to produce it, and *for whom* to produce.

These decisions involve opportunity costs. An *opportunity cost* is what is sacrificed to implement an alternative action, i.e., what is given up to produce or obtain a particular good or service. For example, the opportunity cost of expanding a country's military arsenal is the decreased production of nonmilitary goods and services. Opportunity costs are found in every situation in which scarcity necessitates decision making.

Opportunity cost is the value—monetary or otherwise—of the next best alternative, or that which is given up. This concept is used in both macroeconomics and microeconomics.

Production-Possibility Frontier

A production-possibility frontier shows the maximum number of alternative combinations of goods and services that a society can produce at a given time when there is full utilization of economic resources and technology. Table 1.2 presents alternative combinations of guns and butter output for a hypothetical economy (guns represent the output of military goods, while butter represents nonmilitary goods and services). In choosing what to produce, decision makers have a choice of producing, for example, alternative C—5,000 guns and 14 million units of butter—or any other alternative presented.

Table 1.2

Alternative Outputs	Guns (thousand units)	Butter (million units)
A	0	20
B	2	18
C	5	14
D	9	6
E	10	0

This production-possibility schedule is plotted in Figure 1-2. The curve, labeled PP, is called the production-possibility frontier. Point C plots the combination of 5,000 guns and 14 million units of butter, assuming full employment of the economy's resources and full use of its technology, as do all of the alternatives presented in Table 1.2.

The production-possibility frontier depicts not only limited productive capability and therefore the problem of scarcity, but also the concept of opportunity cost. When an economy is situated on the production-possibility frontier, such as at point C, gun production can be increased only by decreasing butter output. Thus, to move from alternative C (5,000 guns and 14 million units of butter) to alternative D (9,000 guns and 6 million units of butter), the opportunity cost of the additional 4,000 units of gun production is the 8 million less units of butter that are produced.

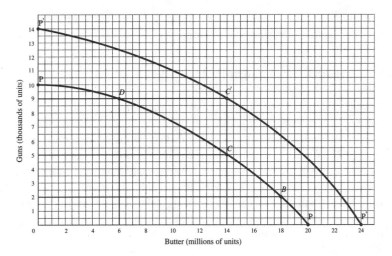

Figure 1-2

The production-possibility frontier shifts outward over time as more resources become available and/or technology is improved. Growth in an economy's productive capability is depicted in Figure 1-2 by the outward shift of the production-possibility frontier from PP to P'P'. Suppose a society chooses to be at point C. When the production-possibility frontier shifts outward, 4,000 additional guns can be produced without sacrificing any butter production, as seen at C'. This example should not be construed as a refutation of the law of opportunity cost just because fewer sacrifices may be made when growth occurs. When there is full utilization of resources and an absence of growth, additional gun production is possible only when the output of butter is decreased.

Points on a production-possibility frontier are considered to be efficient. Points within the frontier are inefficient, and points outside the frontier are unattainable. Points C and D are efficient because all available resources are utilized and there is full use of existing technology. Positions outside the production-possibility frontier are unattainable since the frontier defines the maximum amount that can be produced at a given time. Positions within the frontier are inefficient because some resources are either unemployed or underemployed.

Principle of Increasing Costs

Resources are not equally efficient in the production of all goods and services, i.e., they are not equally productive when used to produce an alternative good. This imperfect substitutability of resources is due to differences in the skills of labor and to the specialized function of most machinery and many buildings. Thus, when the decision is made to produce more guns and less butter, the new resources allocated to the production of guns are usually less productive. It therefore follows that as larger amounts of resources are transferred from the production of butter to the production of guns, increasing units of butter are given up for fewer incremental units of guns. This increasing opportunity cost of gun production illustrates the principle of increasing costs.

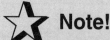 **Note!**

The principle of increasing opportunity cost is the reason why the production-possibility frontier is bowed outward from the origin of the graph, and not a straight line.

Scarcity and the Market System

As we have seen, two of the most important economic decisions faced by a society are deciding what goods and services to produce and how to allocate resources among their competing uses. The combination of goods and services produced can be resolved by government command or through a market system. In a command economy, a central planning board determines the mix of output. The experience with this system, however, has not been very successful, as evidenced by the changing economic and political events in the 1990s in the command economies of Eastern Europe and the former USSR.

In a market economy, economic decisions are decentralized and are made by the collective wisdom of the marketplace, i.e., prices resolve the three fundamental economic questions of what, how, and for whom. The only goods and services produced are those that individuals are willing to purchase at a price sufficient to cover the cost of producing them. Because resources are scarce, goods and services are produced using the technique and resource combination that minimizes the cost of production. And the goods and services produced are sold (distributed) to those who are willing and have the money to pay the prices.

Most countries have a mixed economy, a mixture of both command and market economies. For example, the United States has primarily a market economy, although the government produces some goods, such as roads, and finances these expenditures by taxing the income of individuals and businesses. The government may also regulate how the market operates, such as with minimum wage laws.

True or False Questions

1. Economic models and theories are accurate statements of reality.

2. In the statement "consumption is a function of disposable income," consumption is the dependent variable.

3. Graphs provide a visual representation of the relationship between two variables.

4. A production-possibility frontier depicts the unlimited wants of a society.

5. When there is full employment, the decision to produce more of one good necessitates decreased production of another good.

6. There are increasing costs of production because economic resources are not equally efficient in the production of all goods and services.

Answers: 1. False; 2. True; 3. True; 4. False; 5. True; 6. True

Solved Problems

Solved Problem 1.1 What are some of the problems associated with the study of economics?

Solution: Multiple difficulties may arise with the study of economics.

a. Generalizing from individual experiences often leads to wrong conclusions (this is called the fallacy of composition). For example, an individual becomes richer by increasing his savings, but society as a whole may become poorer if everyone saves because people may be put out of work.

b. The fact that one economic event precedes another does not necessarily imply cause and effect, which is what economists want to study. For example, the U.S. stock market collapse in 1929 did not cause the worldwide Great Depression of the 1930s.

c. Since economics is a social science and laboratory experiments cannot be conducted, economic theories can only describe expected behavior. Thus, these theories are not as precise or reliable as the natural laws established in the pure sciences.

Solved Problem 1.2

a. The demand for purchasing videos might be presented as a function of the video's purchase price. Does this mean that income and the cost of renting a video are unimportant?

b. What is the meaning of and the economist's use of the term *ceteris paribus*?

Solution:

a. To further simplify the demand-for-videos function—$Q_{videos} = f(Y_d, P_{videos}, P_{rental})$—we could assume that the individual's disposable income and the cost of renting videos are unchanged. Thus, while income and rental cost do influence the demand for videos, here more videos are purchased only because of a lower price.

b. The phrase *ceteris paribus* means that other independent variables affecting the dependent variable are held constant, or are unchanged. When other independent variables that influence the quantity of videos purchased are held constant, the demand for videos can be presented as $Q_{videos} = f(P_{videos})$, *ceteris paribus*.

Solved Problem 1.3 Suppose an economy has the production-possibility frontier depicted in Figure 1-3?

a. What implication does the selection of point A or C have regarding the economy's current and future production of consumer goods and services?

b. What linkage is there between saving and economic growth?

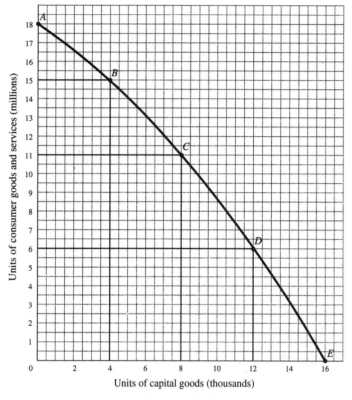

Figure 1-3

Solution:

a. At point *A*, society has more consumer goods and services in the current period. Point *C*, however, provides the possibility of a larger quantity of consumer goods and services in the future because of additions to the economy's stock of capital resources. Here the economy's productive capabilities and thus production-possibilities frontier will expand (perhaps through the addition of a new factory) and thereby provide an increased output of consumer goods and services in a future period.

b. As discussed in a., society must forgo purchases of consumer goods and services now if it is to increase its capital and thereby expand production capabilities. Thus, people must be willing to save, and have fewer goods and services now, so that resources can be used in the current period to produce capital goods.

Solved Problem 1.4 Figure 1-4 presents a production-possibility frontier for food and clothing.

a. What is the opportunity cost of increasing food production from 0 to 2 million units, from 2 million to 4 million units, and from 4 million to 6 million units?

b. What is happening to the opportunity cost of increasing food production from 0 to 6 million units?

c. Explain how the shape of the production-possibility frontier implies increasing costs for the production of clothing.

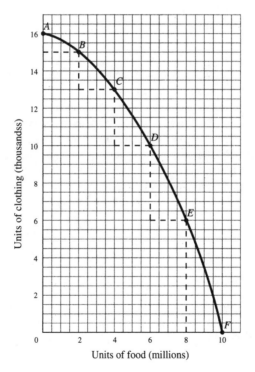

Figure 1-4

Solution:

a. In increasing food production from 0 to 2 million units, production of clothing decreases from 16,000 to 15,000 units. Thus, the opportunity cost of producing the first 2 million units of food is 1 thousand units of clothing. The opportunity cost of a second and third additional 2 million units is 2,000 and 3,000 units of clothing, respectively.

b. The opportunity cost of increasing food production is increasing from 1,000 units of clothing to 2,000 to 3,000 units of clothing.

c. Increasing clothing and food costs are reflected in a concave (outward-sloping) production-possibility frontier. Moving down the frontier from point *A* to points *B*, *C*, *D*, *E*, and *F* shows that to produce 2 million incremental units of food (the 2-million-unit-length horizontal dashed lines in Figure 1-4), we must give up more and more units of clothing (the vertical dashed lines of increasing length).

Solved Problem 1.5 Explain how division of labor and specialization enhance production in an advanced society.

Solution:
Through the division of labor and specialization, the population within a given geographic region, instead of being self-sufficient and producing the full range of goods and services wanted, can concentrate its energies and time in the production of only a few goods and services in which its efficiency is greatest. Thus, specialization and division of labor allow greater output. By then exchanging some of the goods and services so produced for different goods and services produced similarly within a different geographic region, the regions' populations as a whole end up consuming a larger number and greater diversity of goods and services than would otherwise be the case.

Chapter 2
DEMAND, SUPPLY, AND EQUILIBRIUM

Demand

The demand schedule for an individual specifies the units of a good or service that the individual is willing and able to purchase at alternative prices during a given period of time. The relationship between price and quantity demanded is inverse: more units are purchased at lower prices because of a substitution effect and an income effect. As a commodity's price falls, an individual normally purchases more of this good since he or she is like-

ly to substitute it for other goods whose price has remained unchanged. Also, when a commodity's price falls, the purchasing power of an individual with a given income increases, allowing for greater purchases of the commodity. When graphed, the inverse relationship between price and quantity demanded appears as a negatively sloped demand curve. A market demand schedule specifies the units of a good or service all individuals in the market are willing and able to purchase at alternative prices, i.e., $Q_d = f(P)$.

Example 2.1

Table 2.1 gives an individual's demand and the market demand for a commodity. Column 2 shows one individual's demand for corn—the bushels of corn that one individual is willing and able to buy per month at alternative prices. We find, for example, that the individual buys 3.5 bushels of corn each month when the price is $5 per bushel. If there are 1,000 individuals in the market, the market demand for corn is the sum of the quantities the 1,000 individuals will buy at each price. So for example, 1,000 individuals collectively are willing to purchase 3,500 bushels of corn each month at $5 per bushel. The market demand is shown in the last column, which shows the typical relationship between quantity demanded and price, i.e., more units of a commodity are demanded at lower prices. The market demand for corn is plotted in Figure 2-1 and the curve is labeled D. Note that the demand curve is negatively sloped.

The market demand for a good or service is influenced not only by the commodity's price, but also by the price of other goods and services,

Table 2.1

Price (P) ($ per bu)	Quantity Demanded (q) by One Individual (bu per month)	Quantity Demanded (Q) in the Market (1000 individuals) (bu per month)
5	3.5	3500
4	4.5	4500
3	6.0	6000
2	8.0	8000
1	11.0	11,000

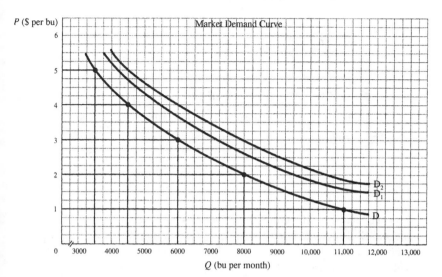

Figure 2-1

disposable income, wealth, tastes, and the size of the market. In presenting the market demand for corn of Table 2.1 and Figure 2-1, variables other than the commodity's price are held constant. This relationship is presented as $Q_d = f(P_{corn})$, *ceteris paribus*, where *ceteris paribus* indicates that variables other than the price of corn are unchanged. When one or more of these variables change, there is a change in demand and therefore a shift of the demand curve. For example, the market demand curve shifts up and to the right when there is an increased preference for the commodity, when income increases, and when the price of a substitute commodity rises and/or the price of a complementary good declines. A substitute good can be used instead of the good considered (wheat for corn), and a complementary good is used together with the good considered (butter with corn).

A common error made by the beginning economics student is failure to differentiate between a change in demand and a change in quantity demanded. A change in demand refers to a shift of the demand curve because a variable other than price has changed. A change in quantity demanded occurs when there is a change in the commodity's price, resulting in a movement along an existing demand curve.

Remember

There is a distinct difference between demand and quantity demanded, and the two must not be
confused.

Example 2.2

The market demand for corn from Table 2.1 was plotted in Figure 2-1 and
labeled D. The market demand shifts up and to the right from D to D_1
when the market size increases—for example, when the number of individuals in this market increases from 1,000 to 1,200. Should the price of
wheat then increase—and individuals substitute corn for wheat in their
diets—the market demand curve for corn again shifts up and to the right,
this time from D_1 to D_2.

Supply

A supply schedule specifies the units of a good or service that a producer is willing to supply (Q_s) at alternative prices over a given period of
time, i.e, $Q_s = f(P)$. The supply curve normally has a positive (upward)
slope, indicating that the producer must receive a higher price for increased output due to the principle of increasing costs. (Review Chapter
1). A market supply curve is derived by summing the units each individual producer is willing to supply at alternative prices. A typical market
supply curve (labeled S) is plotted in Figure 2-2.

The market supply curve shifts when the number and/or size of producers changes, factor prices (wages, interest, and/or rent paid to economic resources) change, the cost of materials changes, technological
progress occurs, and/or the government subsidizes or taxes output.

The market supply curve shifts down and to the right with more producers entering the market, decreases in factor or materials prices, improvement in technology, and government subsidization. A change in
supply thereby denotes a shift of the supply curve. A change in quantity

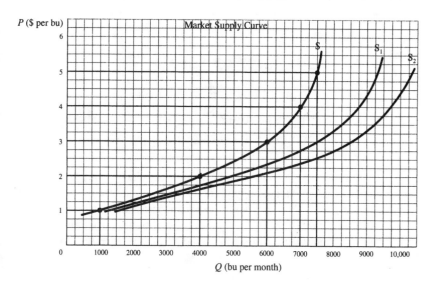

Figure 2-2

supplied indicates a change in the commodity's price and therefore a movement along an existing supply curve. In Figure 2-2, if the number of producers increases, the market supply curve shifts down and to the right from S to S_1. If a technological improvement in corn production also develops, the market supply curve shifts further downward from S_1 to S_2.

Equilibrium Price and Quantity

Equilibrium occurs at the intersection of the market supply and market demand curves. At this intersection, quantity demanded equals quantity supplied, i.e., the quantity that individuals are willing to purchase exactly equals the quantity producers are willing to supply. A surplus exists at prices higher than the equilibrium price since the quantity demanded falls short of the quantity supplied. At prices lower than the equilibrium price, there is a shortage of output since quantity demanded exceeds quantity supplied. Once achieved, the equilibrium price and quantity persist until there is a change in demand and/or supply.

You Need to Know ✔

Economists spend much time and effort in analyzing where and how market equilibrium is achieved. Its importance cannot be overstated.

Equilibrium price and/or equilibrium quantity change when the market demand and/or market supply curves shift. Equilibrium price and equilibrium quantity both rise when there is an increase in market demand with no change in the market supply curve. Equilibrium price falls while equilibrium quantity increases when market supply increases and demand is unchanged.

Government and Price Determination

The government may intervene in the market and mandate a maximum price (price ceiling) or minimum price (price floor) for a good or service. For example, some city governments in the U.S. legislate the maximum price that a landlord can charge a tenant for rent. Such rent-control policies, though well-intentioned, result in a disequilibrium in the housing market since, at the government-mandated price ceiling, the quantity of housing supplied falls short of the quantity of housing demanded. An example of minimum prices (price floors) in the U.S. is the minimum wage. Price floors result in market disequilibrium in that quantity supplied at the mandated price exceeds quantity demanded.

The government can alter an equilibrium price by changing market demand and/or market supply. The government can restrict demand by rationing a good, as occurred for many items during World War II. Equilibrium price can be altered by shifting the market supply curve. A tax on a good raises its supply price—shifts the market supply curve up and to the left—and causes the equilibrium price to increase and the equilibrium quantity to fall. A subsidy to the producer will do the opposite and lower equilibrium price and raise equilibrium quantity.

Elasticity

Market prices will change whenever shifts in supply or demand occur.

Example 2.3

Table 2.2 gives a hypothetical market demand and supply schedule for wheat; it shows whether a surplus or shortage occurs at each price and indicates the pressure on price toward equilibrium. Thus, the equilibrium price is $2 because the quantity demanded, 4,500 bushels of wheat per month, equals the quantity supplied.

Table 2.2

Price ($ per bu)	Quantity Demanded in the Market (1000 bu per month)	Quantity Supplied in the Market (1000 bu per month)	Surplus (+) or Shortage (−)	Pressure on Price
$4	2.0	7.0	+5	downward
3	3.0	6.0	+3	downward
2	4.5	4.5	0	equilibrium
1	6.5	2.5	−4	upward

The elasticity of demand (E_D) measures the percentage change in the quantity demanded of a commodity as a result of a given percentage in its price. The formula is

$$E_D = \frac{\text{percentage change in the quantity demanded}}{\text{percentage change in price}}$$

E_D can be calculated in terms of the new quantity and price, or with the original quantity and price. However, different results would then be obtained. To avoid this problem, economists generally measure E_D in terms of the average quantity and the average price, as follows:

$$E_D = \frac{\text{change in quantity demanded}}{(\text{sum of quantities demanded})/2} \div \frac{\text{change in price}}{(\text{sum of prices})/2}$$

E_D is a pure number. Thus, it is a better measurement tool than the slope, which is expressed in terms of the units of measurement. E_D is always expressed as a positive number, even though price and quantity demand-ed move in opposite directions. The demand curve is said to be elastic if $E_D > 1$, unitary elastic if $E_D = 1$, and inelastic if $E_D < 1$.

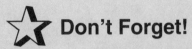

Don't Forget!

Different formulas are used to compute elasticity and slope. A simple glance at a graph is not enough to determine whether a curve has a high or low elasticity.

Example 2.4

The elasticity between the quantities demanded at \$4 and \$3 of Table 2.2 is calculated below using the average quantities and prices.

$$E_D = \frac{1}{(2+3)/2} \div \frac{1}{(4+3)/2} = \frac{1}{2.5} \div \frac{1}{3.5} = \frac{3.5}{2.5} = 1.4$$

Thus, we say that this demand curve is elastic (on the average) be-tween these two points. The elasticity of demand is greater (1) the greater the number of good substitutes available, (2) the greater the proportion of income spent on the commodity, and (3) the longer the time period con-sidered.

When the price of a commodity falls, the total revenue of producers (price times quantity) increases if $E_D > 1$, remains unchanged if $E_D = 1$, and decreases if $E_D < 1$. This occurs because when $E_D > 1$, the percent-age increase in quantity exceeds the percentage *decline* in price and so total revenue (TR) increases. When $E_D = 1$, the percentage increase in quantity equals the percentage decline in price and so TR remains un-changed. Finally, when $E_D < 1$, the percentage increase in quantity is less than the percentage decline in price, and so TR falls.

The *elasticity of supply* (E_S) measures the percentage change in the quantity supplied of a commodity as a result of a given percentage change in its price. We again use the average quantity and price as follows:

$$E_S = \frac{\text{change in quantity supplied}}{(\text{sum of quantities supplied})/2} \div \frac{\text{change in price}}{(\text{sum of prices})/2}$$

E_S is a pure number and is positive because price and quantity move in the same direction. Supply is said to be elastic if $E_S > 1$, unitary elastic if $E_S = 1$, and inelastic if $E_S < 1$.

Example 2.5

The (average) elasticity between the quantities supplied at $1 and $2 of the supply schedule of Table 2.2 is

$$E_S = \frac{2}{(2.5+4.5)/2} \div \frac{1}{(1+2)/2} = \frac{1}{3.5} \div \frac{1}{1.5} \cong 0.43.$$

True or False Questions

1. There is a decrease in the demand for a commodity when the price of a substitute commodity increases.
2. When the supply curve is positively sloped, an increase in demand will result in a larger quantity supplied.
3. A surplus exists when the market price is above the equilibrium price.
4. Government subsidization of firms producing Good A results in an increase in the demand for Good A.
5. Demand is inelastic if the percentage increase in quantity exceeds the percentage decrease in price.
6. A decline in price leaves total revenue unchanged when $E_D = 1$.

Answers: 1. False; 2. True; 3. True; 4. False; 5. False; 6. True

Solved Problems

Solved Problem 2.1 Explain what happens to the demand curve for air transportation between New York City and Washington, D.C., as a result of the following events:

a. The income of households in metropolitan New York and Washington, D.C., increases 20%.

b. The cost of a train ticket between New York City and Washington, D.C., is reduced 50%.

c. The price of an airline ticket decreases 20%.

Solution:

a. Individuals will travel more since they have more disposable income. The demand for air transportation between NYC and Washington increases; the demand curve shifts up and to the right.

b. The cost of an alternative mode of transportation between NYC and Washington has decreased; thus, more individuals will travel by train between NYC and Washington. The demand for air transportation decreases; the demand curve shifts down and to the left.

c. There is no shift, but there is a movement down the existing demand curve; the lower price for an airline ticket results in an increase in the number of people traveling (quantity demanded) by air between NYC and Washington.

Solved Problem 2.2 Suppose the market supply and demand curves for Good A are initially S and D, respectively, in Figure 2-3; equilibrium price is $3 and equilibrium quantity is 280 units.

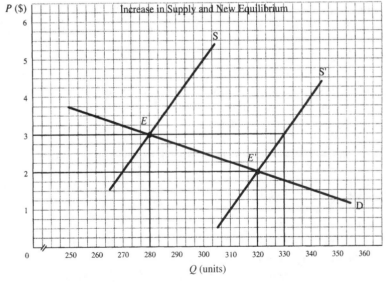

Figure 2-3

a. Suppose improved technology in the production of Good A shifts the market supply curve from S to S', *ceteris paribus*. After the initial supply shift, what is the relationship between quantity demanded and quantity supplied at the initial $3 equilibrium price?

b. What is the new equilibrium price and quantity after the technological advance has increased the supply of Good A?

Solution:

a. Quantity demanded for market schedule D is 280 units when the price is $3, while market supply is 330 units. There is a surplus of Good A at the initial $3 equilibrium price which puts downward pressure on the price of Good A.

b. Equilibrium price falls from $3 to $2 as a result of the increase in market supply; equilibrium quantity increases from 280 to 320 units.

Solved Problem 2.3 Why has the federal government placed price floors on some agricultural goods?

Solution: A price floor is a government-mandated price that exists above the market's equilibrium price; price floors result in a surplus of production. While market demand for most agricultural commodities is relatively stable over time, market supply is very much influenced by the weather. A drought, for example, decreases supply and pushes up prices while a bumper crop can severely depress agricultural prices. The profitability of farming becomes uncertain, as does the price of food products and the income needed to feed a household. Thus, the reasons for agricultural price supports (price floors) are: (1) to stabilize farmer incomes and encourage farmers to continue farming whether there are bumper crops or droughts; (2) to provide a steadier flow of agricultural products at relatively stable prices; and (3) to stabilize the amount of income that households need to spend on food.

Solved Problem 2.4

a. Is the demand for table salt elastic or inelastic? Why?

b. Is the demand for stereos elastic or inelastic? Why?

Solution:

a. The demand for salt is inelastic because there are no good substitutes for salt and households spend a very small portion of their total income on this commodity. Even if the price of salt were to rise substantially, households would reduce their purchases of salt little.

b. The demand for stereos is elastic because stereos are expensive and, as a luxury rather than a necessity, their purchase can be postponed or avoided when their price rises. One could also use the radio as a partial substitute for a stereo.

Solved Problem 2.5

a. Should the price of a subway ride or bus ride be increased or decreased if total revenue needs to be increased?

b. What about the price of a taxi ride?

Solution:

a. To the extent that there are no inexpensive good substitutes for public transportation in metropolitan areas, the demand for subway and bus rides is inelastic. Their prices should, therefore, be increased to increase total revenue. However, this can be self-defeating. Sharply increasing the price of public transportation will encourage people to use their cars and increase congestion and pollution.

b. For taxi rides, the case is likely to be different. Taxi rides are relatively expensive; an increase in their price may encourage people to rely much more on their cars and public transportation. To the extent that this makes the demand for taxi rides elastic, total revenue will fall when the price of taxi rides is increased.

Chapter 3
UNEMPLOYMENT, INFLATION, AND NATIONAL INCOME

IN THIS CHAPTER:

- ✔ *Gross Domestic Output*
- ✔ *Aggregate Demand, Aggregate Supply, and Equilibrium Output*
- ✔ *Changes in Aggregate Output*
- ✔ *Business Cycles*
- ✔ *Unemployment and the Labor Force*
- ✔ *Inflation*
- ✔ *True or False Questions*
- ✔ *Solved Problems*

Gross Domestic Output

Gross domestic product (GDP) measures total output in the domestic economy. Nominal GDP, real GDP, and potential GDP are three different measures of aggregate output. *Nominal GDP* is the market value of all final goods and services produced in the domestic economy in a one-year period *at current prices*. By this definition, (1) only output exchanged in a market is included (do-it-yourself services such as cleaning your own house are not included); (2) output is valued in its final form (output is in its final form when no further alteration is made to the good which would change its market value); and (3) output is measured using current-year prices.

Because nominal GDP values are inflated by prices that increase over time, aggregate output is also measured holding the prices of all goods and services constant over time. This valuation of GDP *at constant prices* is called *real GDP*.

The third measure of aggregate output is *potential GDP*, the maximum production that can take place in the domestic economy without putting upward pressure on the general level of prices. Conceptually, potential GDP represents a point on a given production-possibility frontier.

The U.S. economy's potential output increases at a fairly steady rate each year while actual real GDP fluctuates around potential GDP. These fluctuations of real GDP are identified as business cycles. The GDP gap is the difference between potential GDP and real GDP; it is positive when potential GDP exceeds real GDP and negative when real GDP exceeds potential GDP. A positive gap indicates that there are unemployed resources and the economy is operating inefficiently within its production-possibility frontier. It therefore follows that an economy's rate of unemployment rises as its GDP gap increases, and falls when the gap declines. An economy is operating above its normal productive capacity when there is a negative gap.

Aggregate Demand, Aggregate Supply, and Equilibrium Output

The economy's equilibrium level of output occurs at the point of intersection of aggregate supply and aggregate demand. In microeconomics, equilibrium price exists where quantity demanded equals quantity supplied. The supply and demand schedules in macroeconomics differ in that they relate the aggregate quantity supplied and the aggregate quantity demanded to the price level.

Important Things to Remember

Supply and demand curves may appear similar to aggregate supply and aggregate demand curves in graphs, but they are substantially different.

An aggregate demand curve represents the collective spending of consumers, businesses, and government, as well as net foreign purchases of goods and services, at different price levels. An aggregate demand curve, like the demand curve in microeconomics, is negatively related to price, holding constant other factors that influence aggregate spending decisions.

Price, presented as *price level* in macroeconomics, affects aggregate spending because of an interest rate effect, a wealth effect, and an international purchasing power effect. The interest rate effect traces the effect that interest rate levels have upon aggregate spending. The nominal rate of interest is directly related to the price level, *ceteris paribus*. Increases in the price level push up interest rates, which usually will depress interest-sensitive spending. The wealth effect relates changes in wealth to changes in aggregate spending. The market value of many financial assets falls as price level and interest rates increase. A higher price level will decrease the household sector's net wealth, lower consumer spending, and cause lower aggregate spending. A country's imports and exports are also affected by a changing price level, i.e., by an international purchasing power effect. When the price level increases in the home country and is unchanged in foreign countries, foreign-made commodities become relatively less expensive, the home country's exports fall, its imports increase, and there is less aggregate spending on the home country's output.

An aggregate demand curve shifts when there is a change in a variable (other than price level) that affects aggregate spending decisions. Outward shifts (to the right) occur when consumers become more willing to spend or there are increases in investment spending, government expenditures, and net exports. Determinants of these factors will be taken up in the next chapter.

An aggregate supply schedule depicts the relationship of aggregate output and price level, holding constant other variables that could affect supply. There is some disagreement among economists on the shape of the aggregate supply curve. Three distinct curves can characterize this disagreement. The Keynesian aggregate supply curve is horizontal until it reaches the economy's full-employment level of output, at which point it becomes positively sloped. Others view the aggregate supply curve as always being positively sloped. The classical aggregate supply curve is vertical at the full-employment level, indicating there is no relationship between aggregate output and the price level.

Changes in economy-wide resource availability, resource cost, and technology shift the aggregate supply curve. The aggregate supply curve shifts rightward when (1) improved technology increases the potential output of a given quantity of resources; (2) the quantity of economic resources increases; or (3) the cost of resources declines.

Changes in Aggregate Output

The effect of changes in aggregate demand and/or aggregate supply upon equilibrium output and the price level depends upon the shape of the aggregate supply curve. With a Keynesian aggregate supply curve, an increase in aggregate demand affects only output as long as the economy is below full-employment output, whereas an increase in aggregate supply has no effect upon either the price level or output. Increases in aggregate demand and/or aggregate supply affect both the price level and real output when aggregate supply is positively sloped, as can be seen in Figure 3-1. For a classical aggregate supply curve, increases in aggregate demand result in only a higher price level, whereas increases in aggregate supply result in a higher level of output and a lower price level.

Example 3.1

Equilibrium real output is y_1 and the price level is p_1 for aggregate supply and aggregate demand curves AS' and AD' in Figure 3-1. Increased government spending shifts the aggregate demand curve outward to AD″, and the point of equilibrium changes from E_1 to E_2. Equilibrium output increases from y_1 to y_2 as the price level rises from p_1 to p_2. When aggregate supply increases to AS″ and aggregate demand remains at AD′,

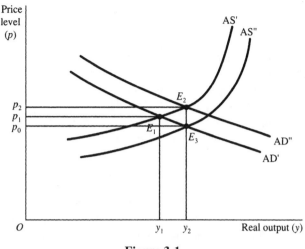

Figure 3-1

the equilibrium point changes from point E_1 to E_3. Equilibrium output increases from y_1 to y_2 and the price level falls from p_1 to p_0.

There are two approaches to measuring aggregate output: an expenditure approach, which measures the value of final sales, and a cost approach, which measures the value added in producing final output. The expenditure or final sales approach consists of summing the consumption spending of individuals (C), investment spending by businesses (I), government expenditures (G), and net exports (X_n). [$GDP = C + I + G + X_n$]. The cost approach consists of summing the value added to final output at each stage of production. Gross domestic product consists of all output produced within the country's boundaries.

Business Cycles

A business cycle is a cumulative fluctuation in aggregate output that lasts for some time. Although recurrent, the duration and intensity of each fluctuation varies. Points at which aggregate output changes direction are marked by peaks and troughs. A *peak* is a point which marks the end of economic expansion (rising aggregate output) and the beginning of a recession (decline in economic activity). A *trough* marks the end of a recession and the beginning of economic recovery. The time span between troughs and peaks is classified as an expansionary period (trough to peak) or a contractionary period (peak to trough).

There are a number of explanations for the cyclical behavior of aggregate output. The central focus of many of these theories is investment spending and consumer purchases of durable goods. These expenditures consist of large-ticketed items whose purchase, in most cases, can be postponed. For example, an individual can repair an existing car rather than purchase a new one. Thus, purchases of such items occur when credit (borrowing) is more readily available or less costly, individuals are more optimistic about the future, and/or cash flows are more certain. However no one theory is able to explain why some business cycles are more severe than others. This suggests that there are numerous causes and that the importance of each cause varies.

Unemployment and the Labor Force

The U.S. labor force does not include the entire population but only those who are at least 16 years old, employed, or unemployed and looking for work. A working-age person who is not looking for work is considered voluntarily unemployed and is not included in the labor force. Thus, the size of the labor force and the number of people unemployed can be understated when a significant number of workers, after some searching, become discouraged and stop looking for work.

The unemployment rate is the percent of the total labor force that is unemployed. Unemployment arises for frictional, structural, and cyclical reasons. Frictional unemployment is temporary and occurs when a person (1) quits a current job before securing a new one, (2) is not immediately hired when entering the labor force, or (3) is let go by a dissatisfied employer. Workers who lose their jobs due to a change in the demand for a particular commodity or because of technological advance are structurally unemployed; their unemployment normally lasts for a longer period since they usually possess specialized skills which are not demanded by other employers. Cyclical unemployment is the result of insufficient aggregate demand. Workers have the necessary skills and are available to work, but there are insufficient jobs because of inadequate aggregate spending. Cyclical unemployment occurs when real GDP falls below potential GDP.

 **Note!**

In the economist's definition of unemployment, not everyone that is without a job is unemployed.

Full employment exists when there is no cyclical unemployment but normal amounts of frictional and structural unemployment; thus, full employment exists at an unemployment rate greater than zero. This is referred to as the natural rate of unemployment. It may change when there is a change in the normal amount of frictional and structural unemployment. The cyclical unemployment rate can be negative when real GDP exceeds potential GDP and the economy is producing beyond its normal full-employment level. This negative cyclical unemployment rate indicates that the normal job search period for the frictionally and structurally unemployed is shortened because of an abnormally large number of job openings. Cyclical unemployment imposes costs upon both society and the person unemployed. Society's opportunity cost is the amount of output which is not produced and therefore is lost forever. The personal costs that occur during an economic downturn are unevenly distributed between different types of workers.

Example 3.2

Table 3.1 presents the unemployment rate by sex, age, and race in 1992, when U.S. real GDP was considerably below potential output, and in 1987, when U.S. real GDP equaled potential GDP. Note that the unemployment rate is always higher for teenagers than for those older, and higher for blacks and others than for whites. This difference worsens when the economy is below its potential GDP.

Inflation

A price index relates prices in a specific year, month, or quarter to prices during a reference period. For example, the *consumer price index* (CPI), the most frequently quoted price index, relates the prices that urban consumers paid for a fixed basket of approximately 400 goods and services

Table 3.1

Demographic Group	1992	1987
All civilian workers	7.4	6.2
By age:		
16–19	20.0	16.9
All males 16–19	21.5	17.8
All females 16–19	18.5	15.9
Males 20 and older	6.9	5.4
Females 20 and older	6.3	5.4
By race:		
White	6.5	5.3
Black and other	12.7	11.6
By sex:		
Female	6.9	6.2
Male	7.8	6.2

SOURCE: *Economic Report of the President, 1994*

in a given month to the prices that existed during a reference period. The *producer price index* (PPI) and GDP deflator are the other two major price indexes. The PPI measures the prices for finished goods, intermediate materials, and crude materials at the wholesale level. Because wholesale prices are even-  tually translated into retail prices, changes in the PPI are usually a good predictor of changes in the CPI. The *GDP deflator* is the most comprehensive measure of the price level since it measures prices for net exports, investment, and government expenditures, as well as for consumer spending.

Inflation is the annual rate of increase in the price level. *Disinflation* is a term used to denote a slowdown in the rate of inflation; deflation exists when there is an annual rate of decrease in the price level. While there have been some monthly decreases in the price level, the U.S. economy has not experienced deflation since the 1930s.

You Need to Know ✔

Inflation refers to an increase in the general price level, not the price of a specific good or service.

Economists identify two distinct causes of inflation. *Demand-pull inflation* is inflation that occurs when aggregate spending exceeds the economy's normal full-employment level of output, i.e., when aggregate demand is pushed too far to the right along a given aggregate supply curve. Demand-pull inflation is normally characterized by both a rising price and output level. It often results in an unemployment rate lower than the natural rate. *Cost-push inflation* originates from increases in the cost of producing goods and services, such as wages or the prices of raw materials. Aggregate supply is pushed to the left, which is referred to as *stagflation*. It is associated with increases in the price level, decreases in aggregate output, and an increase in the unemployment rate above the natural rate.

Inflation can slow economic growth, redistribute income and wealth, and cause economic activity to contract. Inflation impairs decision making since it creates uncertainty about future prices and/or costs and distorts economic values. For example, a business may postpone the purchase of equipment because of increasing uncertainty about the purchasing power of future money streams. Such postponed capital outlays slow capital formation and economic growth.

True or False Questions

1. Increases in nominal GDP always result in increases in real GDP.
2. Increases in a positive GDP gap are associated with increases in the unemployment rate.
3. All economists agree that an increase in aggregate demand will result in an increase in both the price level and real output.
4. A business cycle occurs every two years.
5. Unemployment only imposes a cost upon those who are unemployed.
6. Cyclical unemployment is unevenly distributed among members of the labor force.

Answers: 1. False; 2. True; 3. False; 4. False; 5. False; 6. True

Solved Problems

Solved Problem 3.1
a. Distinguish between a final good and an intermediate good.
b. Is a loaf of bread a final or an intermediate good?

Solution:

a. A final good is one that involves no further processing and is purchased for final use. An intermediate good is one that: (1) involves further processing; (2) is being purchased, modified, and then resold by the purchaser; or (3) is resold during the year for a profit.

b. A loaf of bread could be either a final or intermediate good, depending upon the purchaser's use of the good. It is a final good when purchased by a household for consumption; it is an intermediate good when purchased by a deli which resells the bread as part of a sandwich.

Solved Problem 3.2 An economy's potential output is depicted by the production-possibility frontier in Figure 3-2.

a. Explain the relationship between potential GDP and real GDP when output is at point A.

b. What is a GDP gap?

c. Is there a GDP gap for the situation described in part a?

d. Can a GDP gap be negative?

Solution:

a. Point A is within the economy's production-possibility frontier. Thus, actual output is less than the economy's ability to produce, i.e., real GDP is less than potential GDP.

b. A GDP gap exists when real GDP does not equal potential GDP. It is measured by subtracting real GDP from potential GDP.

c. There is a positive GDP gap at point A since the economy's production of goods and services is below its ability to produce.

d. The production-possibility frontier measures the economy's ability to produce goods and services *without* putting upward pressure on output prices. The production-possibility frontier can thus be exceeded, but in doing so there are increases in both output and the price level. Thus, a negative GDP gap can exist—real GDP can exceed potential GDP—when real GDP is, for example, at point B in Figure 3-2 and the economy is producing beyond its full-employment level of output.

Solved Problem 3.3 Use aggregate demand and aggregate supply curves AD and AS in Figure 3-3 to answer the following questions:

a. Is the aggregate supply curve Keynesian or classical?

b. Find the economy's equilibrium level of output and price level.

c. Does an increase in government spending, *ceteris paribus*, shift

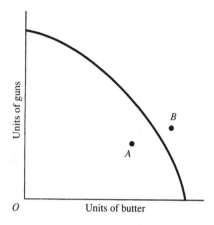

Figure 3-2

aggregate demand or aggregate supply? What happens to equilibrium output and the price level?

d. Suppose there is a technological advance rather than an increase in government spending. What happens to aggregate demand? Aggregate supply? Equilibrium output? The price level?

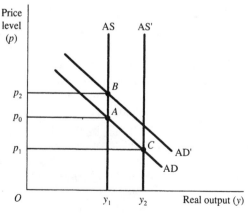

Figure 3-3

Solution:

a. Figure 3-3 depicts a classical aggregate supply curve since it shows no relationship between aggregate output and the price level.

b. Equilibrium exists where the aggregate demand curve intersects the aggregate supply curve. Equilibrium for curves AD and AS exists at point A; the price level is p_0 and output is y_1.

c. Increased government spending results in an outward shift of aggregate demand. There is no change in aggregate supply since there has been no change in the economy's ability to produce goods and services. If aggregate demand shifts from AD to AD', then equilibrium now exists at point B. Equilibrium output remains at y_1 and equilibrium prices increases from p_0 to p_2.

d. The technological advance has no effect on aggregate demand, but it shifts aggregate supply rightward from AS to AS'. Equilibrium changes from point A to point C. Equilibrium output has increased from y_1 to y_2, while the price level has decreased from p_0 to p_1.

Solved Problem 3.4

a. What effect does unanticipated inflation have upon: (1) individuals who are retired and living on a fixed income; (2) debtors, and (3) creditors?

b. How does indexation protect one from the redistribution effect of inflation?

Solution:

a. (1) Unanticipated inflation lowers the real income of those on a fixed income. An increase in the price level reduces the purchasing power of a fixed nominal income; the result is the purchase of fewer goods and services. (2) Debtors benefit from unanticipated inflation since the dollars they pay back have less purchasing power. (3) Creditors (lenders), on the other hand, lose from unanticipated inflation since the dollars they are repaid purchase fewer goods and services.

b. Indexation ties money payments to a price level so that the sum of money payments rises proportionately with the price level. For example, a $20,000 salary would increase to $22,000 when the monetary payments of $20,000 are indexed and there is a 10 percent increase in the price level.

Chapter 4

CONSUMPTION, INVESTMENT, NET EXPORTS, AND GOVERNMENT EXPENDITURES

IN THIS CHAPTER:

- ✔ Consumption
- ✔ Investment
- ✔ Net Exports
- ✔ Government Taxes and Expenditures
- ✔ True or False Questions
- ✔ Solved Problems

Consumption

Because consumption represents two-thirds of total aggregate spending in the U.S., understanding the determinants of consumer spending is central to any analysis of the economy's level of output. Consumer spending is largely determined by personal income, income taxes, consumer expectations, consumer indebtedness, wealth, and price level. Since consumption is impossible for most individuals without income from employment or through transfers from business or government, personal income is the most important of these variables. Personal income taxes are also central in that one's ability to spend depends not upon the income received but on the income available for spending.

A consumption function is the relationship of consumption to disposable income, holding nonincome determinants of consumption constant. Figure 4-1 plots the consumption function for a hypothetical economy, labeled C'. A change in a nonincome determinant of consumption alters the relationship of consumption to disposable income. Such changes are depicted graphically by upward or downward shifts of the consumption function. Shifts of the consumption function affect the level of consumption and saving.

The 45° line in Figure 4-1 is equidistant from both the consumption and disposable income axes. As drawn, $C = Y_d$ at each point on this 45° line. For linear consumption function C', there is only one level of disposable income at which consumer spending equals disposable income, and that is the point of intersection of the consumption line and the 45° line. Since the consumption line is below the 45° line at disposable income levels above $500 billion, it follows that consumers are not consuming their entire income and therefore are saving. Thus, consumer saving is the distance between the consumption line and the 45° line at each level of disposable income.

Example 4.1

Should consumers expect an increase in the price level, they are likely to spend more in the current period before prices rise. An upward shift of consumption function C' to C" in Figure 4-1 results. We now find that at disposable income of $500 billion, consumption exceeds disposable income, i.e., consumers are dissaving. (Consumers can dissave by borrowing or by spending accumulated savings). Consumption now equals disposable income when Y_d is $600 billion; for consumption function C" there is less saving at each level of disposable income than there is for consumption function C'.

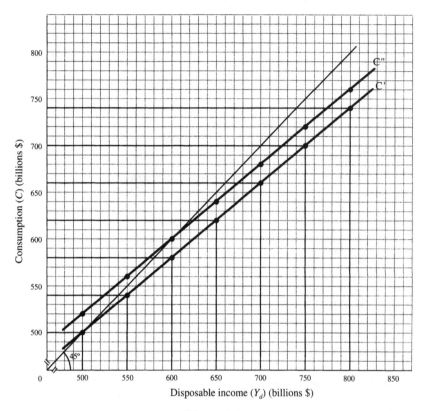

Figure 4-1

The *marginal propensity to consume* is the ratio of the change in consumption relative to the change in disposable income between two levels of disposable income ($MPC = \Delta C / \Delta Y_d$), while the marginal propensity to save is the ratio of the change in saving relative to the change in disposable income ($MPS = \Delta S / \Delta Y_d$). Also $MPS = 1 - MPC$.

Example 4.2

From Figure 4-1, consumption (under C') increases from $500 billion to $540 billion when disposable income increases from $500 billion to $550 billion; the MPC is therefore 0.80 since ΔC of $40 billion divided by ΔY_d

of $50 billion equals 0.80. For consumption function C', the MPC = 0.80 for each change in disposable income. It is constant for any linear consumption function since the MPC is the consumption function's slope, and all straight lines have a constant slope.

Note!

Consumers comprise the largest percentage of aggregate spending, so their actions are very important to the strength of the economy.

Investment

Gross investment is the least stable component of aggregate spending and a principal cause of the business cycle. In calculating GDP, investment consists of residential construction; nonresidential construction (offices, hotels, and other commercial real estate); producers' durable equipment; and changes in inventories. While the rate of interest is only one of many variables that influence investment decisions, it is customary to present investment demand as a negative function of the interest rate, holding constant the other variables which influence the decision to invest. Thus, a lower interest rate is associated with a higher level of investment, and vice versa.

Holding other variables constant, we expect that at a lower rate of interest (1) more households are financially able to carry a mortgage, and a greater number of housing units will be demanded; (2) businesses are more willing and able to purchase durable equipment and to carry larger inventories; and (3) real estate developers find that there are a larger number of purchasers for newly constructed commercial real estate.

Net Exports

Gross exports are the value of goods and services produced in a home country and sold abroad, i.e., they are the value of foreign spending on U.S.-produced goods and services. *Gross imports* are the value of U.S.

purchases of goods and services produced in other countries. When commodities are imported, some of the consumption and gross investment spending is for foreign-produced rather than U.S.-produced goods. Imports thereby lower aggregate spending on domestically produced goods.

Net exports are the value of gross exports less gross imports, i.e., the net addition to domestic aggregate spending that results from importing and exporting goods and services. Net exports are positive when the home country exports more than it imports, and negative when the home country imports more than it exports.

Numerous variables affect a country's imports and exports. A country's imports are related to its level of income, foreign exchange rate, domestic prices relative to prices in foreign countries, import tariffs, and restrictions on imported goods. Exports are influenced by the same variables, except that the income levels of foreign countries rather than that of the home country affect the amount exported. Because these variables change with time, it is reasonable to expect a country's net export balance to change over time.

You Need to Know ✔

In the United States net exports are often referred to as the trade deficit because U.S. imports have been greater than exports for some time.

Government Taxes and Expenditures

Government spending increases when Congress passes legislation authorizing new spending. Tax revenues finance this government spending and government transfer payments to the private sector. Government transfer payments (in the form of unemployment insurance, social security payments, and various government assistance programs) can be viewed as a negative tax. Net tax revenues consist of income taxes plus lump-sum taxes less transfer payments. Net tax revenues fall when transfer payments increase, and rise when greater per capita taxes are imposed.

With respect to income tax receipts, net tax revenues increase when output increases and more taxes are collected or when government imposes a higher income tax rate.

Don't Forget!

Income tax receipts may decrease if the economy slows, not just because Congress cuts tax rates.

True or False Questions

1. A change in disposable income causes an equal change in consumption.
2. Investment spending is the most unstable component of aggregate spending.
3. Consumption and investment spending in the national income accounts is solely for domestically produced goods and services.
4. Imports by a country are unrelated to its level of GDP.

Answers: 1. False; 2. True; 3. False; 4. False

Solved Problems

Solved Problem 4.1 Suppose the economy's consumption function is specified by the equation $C = \$50 + 0.80Y_d$.
   a. Find consumption when disposable income (Y_d) is $400, $500, and $600.
   b. Plot this consumption equation and label it C'.
   c. Use the plotted consumption function to find saving when disposable income is $400, $500, and $600.
   d. What amount of consumption for consumption function C' is autonomous, and what amount is induced when disposable income is $400? $500? $600?

Solution:
   a. Consumption for each level of disposable income is found by substituting the specified disposable income level into the consumption

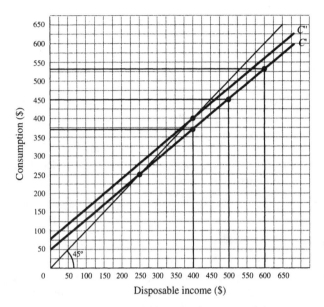

Figure 4-2

equation. Thus, for $Y_d = \$400$, $C = \$50 + 0.80(\$400) = \$50 + \$320 = \$370$. So, C is $450 when $Y_d = \$500$, and $530 when $Y_d = \$600$.

b. The linear consumption function $C = \$50 + 0.80Y_d$ is plotted in Figure 4-2.

c. Saving is the difference between disposable income and consumption. Using the calculation from part a., we find that saving is $30 when Y_d is $400 ($Y_d - C = S = \$400 - \$370 = \$30$), $50 when Y_d is $500, and $70 when Y_d is $600. Saving is the difference between the consumption line and the 45° line at each level of disposable income in Figure 4-2. Thus, reading up from the $400 income level, we find that C is $370; the distance from consumption function C' to the 45° line at the $400 income level is $30—the amount of saving.

d. Autonomous consumption is the amount consumed when disposable income is 0. In Figure 4-2, autonomous consumption is $50, the amount consumed when the consumption line C' intersects the vertical axis and disposable income is 0. Since autonomous consumption is unrelated to income, autonomous consumption is $50 for all levels of income. Induced consumption is the amount of consumption that depends upon the receipt of income. Consumption is $370 when disposable income is $400. Since $50 is consumed regardless of the income level, $320 of the $370 level of consumption is induced by disposable income. Induced consumption is $400 when disposable income is $500, and $480 when disposable income is $600.

Solved Problem 4.2 What will happen to consumption function C' in Figure 4-2 when:

a. Consumers consider their job secure and therefore become more confident about the future level of disposable income?

b. Credit card issuers implement tighter credit standards and consumers are less able to buy goods and services on credit?

c. Consumers expect the price level to increase 10 percent by year end?

Solution:

a. Consumers become more willing to consume their current disposable income. Consumption function C' in Figure 4-2 shifts upward to C'', and consumption is greater for each level of disposable income.

b. Some consumers are no longer able to borrow to purchase goods and services in the current period. The consumption function will shift downward from C'' to C'. Consumption is lower for each level of disposable income.

c. Consumers reschedule future purchases to the current period because of the expected rise in prices for goods and services. Consumption function C' shifts upward to C''.

Solved Problem 4.3 Variables other than the rate of interest affect gross investment. Changes in these other variables cause investment demand to shift downward or upward. What should happen to the economy's investment demand when there is a change in the following variables?

a. There is an increase in consumer confidence.

b. Manufacturers' utilization of existing capacity declines.

c. There is an increase in vacancy rates in commercial buildings.

Solution:

a. Investment demand should shift upward. Housing sales should increase as consumers become more confident; builders would construct more new housing to meet this increased demand.

b. Investment demand should shift downward. Businesses' purchases of durable equipment should fall since such purchases would expand productive capacity and there is no need to expand productive capacity when utilization of existing capacity is declining.

c. Investment demand should shift downward. Increased vacancy rates for existing commercial buildings indicate that there will be difficulty selling newly constructed commercial real estate. Thus, commercial real estate construction will decline.

Solved Problem 4.4 What is the difference between a lump-sum tax and an income tax?

Solution: A lump-sum tax is a fixed-sum tax that is unrelated to income. An income tax is related directly to earned income. In the case of a proportional income tax the government collects a fixed percent of income earned, while for a progressive income tax the rate of taxation increases with the level of income. Lump-sum taxes and proportional and progressive income taxes are illustrated in Figure 4-3. Note that lump-sum taxes remain at $1,000 as income increases from $10,000 to $11,000. When there is a 10 percent proportional income tax rate, tax payments increase from $1,000 to $1,100 as income increases from $10,000 to $11,000. When the tax rate is 10 percent on the first $10,000 earned and 20 percent on income greater than $10,000, tax payments increase from $1,000 to $1,200 when income increases from $10,000 to $11,000.

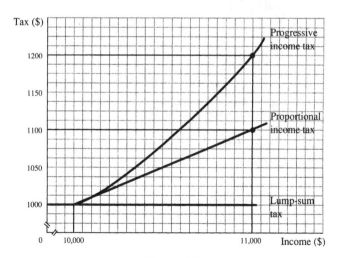

Figure 4-3

Chapter 5

TRADITIONAL KEYNESIAN APPROACH TO EQUILIBRIUM OUTPUT

IN THIS CHAPTER:

- ✔ *Keynesian Model of Equilibrium Output*
- ✔ *Income-Expenditure Model of Equilibrium Output*
- ✔ *Leakage-Injection Model of Equilibrium Output*
- ✔ *The Multiplier*
- ✔ *Changes in Equilibrium Output When Aggregate Supply Is Positively Sloped*

✔ *True or False Questions*

✔ *Solved Problems*

Keynesian Model of Equilibrium Output

John Maynard Keynes developed the framework for modern-day macro-economics in the 1930s. Because there was considerable unemployment at that time, he assumed that changes in aggregate demand have no effect upon the price level as long as output is below the full-employment level, i.e., as long as aggregate supply is horizontal. A positive GDP gap—where real GDP is below potential GDP—is identified as a recessionary gap and is the distance between equilibrium output and full-employment output on an AD-AS graph. An inflationary gap exists when there is excessive aggregate spending, such that aggregate demand intersects the Keynesian aggregate supply curve in the positively sloped region beyond full-employment output. This results in an increase in the price level.

Income-Expenditure Model of Equilibrium Output

The Keynesian model of output can be expressed as a circular flow of income and output between businesses and individuals. In a capitalist, free-market economy, individuals own, directly or indirectly, the economy's economic resources (land, labor, and capital).  Businesses hire resources to produce output and pay individuals a money income for the services of these resources in the form of wages, rent, interest, and profits. Individuals in turn spend their money income and purchase output. Assuming no supply constraints (when aggregate supply is horizontal), we can expect businesses to supply output as long as the receipts from selling output equal the payments made by businesses to the owners of economic resources and the owners of the business firms.

 **Note!**

The circular flow of income and output helps to explain why we should all study economics because one person's actions have repercussions for others.

The circular flow of income and expenditure can be used to find the economy's equilibrium level of output. The market value of final output for a hypothetical economy appears in column 1 of Table 5.1.

Assuming a capitalist system with no government spending or taxes, the value of output in column 1 is also the disposable income of individuals since individuals receive all the payments made to the factors of production. Aggregate spending in column 5 is the sum of consumer spending (column 2), investment spending (column 3), and net exports (column 4). Note that consumer spending increases with the level of output and thus the level of personal disposable income, as discussed in Chapter 4. Investment and net exports are assumed here to be unrelated to the output level and remain constant. The equilibrium level of output is $800 billion since this is the only level of production at which output equals aggregate spending. This equilibrium condition is depicted in col-

Table 5.1
(in Billions of $)

(1) Output (Y)	(2) Consumer Spending (C)	(3) Investment Spending (I)	(4) Net Exports (X_n)	(5) Aggregate Spending ($C + I + X_n$)	(6) Surplus (+)/Shortage (−) $Y - (C + I + X_n)$
650	570	100	10	680	−30
700	610	100	10	720	−20
750	650	100	10	760	−10
800	690	100	10	800	0
850	730	100	10	840	+10
900	770	100	10	880	+20
950	810	100	10	920	+30

umn 6 by the absence of production shortages or surpluses. At output levels below $800 billion there is a shortage of output (aggregate spending is greater than production), while at output levels greater than $800 billion there is surplus production.

The income-expenditure approach to output can be presented graphically beginning with the linear consumption function and the 45° line encountered in Chapter 4. Adding investment spending and net exports shifts the linear consumption function upward to the aggregate spending line $(C + I + X_n)$. Aggregate spending equals output at only one level of output, determined by the intersection of the 45° line and the aggregate spending line. It can be shown that increases (upward shifts) or decreases (downward shifts) of aggregate spending increase or decrease the economy's equilibrium level of output.

Example 5.1

The equilibrium level of output can be found algebraically by equating output and aggregate spending. Suppose the equation for the linear consumption function is $C = \$70 + 0.8Y$; I is $120 and $X_n = 0$. Equilibrium output is found by solving $Y = C + I + X_n$ for Y.

$$Y = C + I + X_n$$
$$Y = \$70 + 0.8Y + \$120 + 0$$
$$Y - 0.8Y = \$70 + \$120 + 0$$
$$0.2Y = \$190$$
$$Y = \$190.2 = \$950$$

Leakage-Injection Model of Equilibrium Output

The leakage-injection model of equilibrium output focuses on saving and gross imports as leakages from the circular flow and on investment and gross exports as spending injections. Leakages depress aggregate spending, while injections increase aggregate spending. For example, spending on domestic output declines when individuals buy more imported rather than domestically produced commodities. An equilibrium level of output exists in the leakage-injection model when the sum of leakages equals the sum of injections.

The paradox of thrift demonstrates that increases or decreases in consumers' desire to save, *ceteris paribus*, affect the economy's output level but not its saving level. Suppose that there are no exports or imports and that the government neither taxes nor spends. Individuals begin to save more of their income, which is a leakage. If investment does not increase, leakages will not equal injections. However, output will be decreased because individuals are not spending as much with more saving. Since output becomes income to individuals, income will decrease until saving equals investment again, i.e., leakages equal injections. If investment does not change, saving must end up at its initial value. Individuals may be saving a greater percentage of their income, but they have less income. So saving stays the same while output decreases. Saving has hurt the economy, thus the paradox.

Remember

The paradox of thrift explains why it is good for an individual to save, but not necessarily good for the economy in general.

The Multiplier

Shifts of the aggregate spending curve result in a change in the equilibrium level of output that is several times larger than the initial shift of the curve. This multiplied effect upon output arises from consumption's positive relationship to income. For example, an increase in investment spending of $10 billion will raise consumers' income by $10 billion, which results in numerous rounds of induced consumer spending. The new recipients of the $10 billion will consume 80 percent or $8 billion (if the MPC = 0.80). This new $8 billion in spending will become new income to individuals who will also spend 80 percent or $6.40 billion, and so on.

⭐ Important!

The multiplier is extremely important in explaining how strong an impact one person's actions can have upon the economy.

The value of the multiplier (k) is found by relating the change in output (ΔY) to the initial change in aggregate spending. The value of the multiplier can also be found from the equation $k = 1/(1 - \text{MPC})$. Thus, the multiplier is 5 if the MPC = 0.80.

Changes in Equilibrium Output When Aggregate Supply Is Positively Sloped

When the aggregate supply curve is positively sloped, increases in aggregate demand raise both equilibrium output and the price level, even though output may be below its full-employment level. The $50 billion outward shift of aggregate demand from AD' to AD" in Figure 5-1 raises equilibrium output $40 billion rather than $50 billion because of a positively sloped aggregate supply curve.

If the aggregate supply curve had been horizontal in this range and the price level had remained at p_1, equilibrium output would have increased $50 billion, an amount equal to the shift in the aggregate demand curve. It therefore follows that an increase in aggregate spending, when aggregate supply is positively sloped, has a smaller multiplier effect since the increase in the price level decreases wealth (which limits the expansion of induced consumer spending), causes higher interest rates (which slow investment spending), and reduces the purchasing power of the home currency (which increases imports and decreases exports).

True or False Questions

1. An inflationary gap exists when output is above the economy's equilibrium level of output.

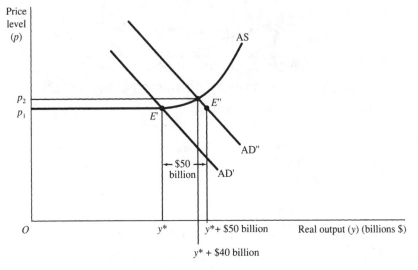

Figure 5-1

2. A production shortage exists when the output level is to the right of the point of intersection of the aggregate spending line and the 45° line.

3. A decrease in saving, *ceteris paribus*, results in a decrease in the equilibrium level of output.

4. A $5 billion increase in investment spending results in a $50 billion increase in the equilibrium level of output when the MPC is 0.90 and aggregate supply is horizontal.

5. An equilibrium level of output exists when output is $550 billion, investment spending is $70 billion, net exports equal $30 billion, and the consumption function is $C = \$10$ billion $+ 0.80Y$.

Answers: 1. False; 2. False; 3. False; 4. True; 5. True

Solved Problems

Solved Problem 5.1 Suppose individuals own all businesses and economic resources, government does not tax or spend, and the business sector produces 500 units at an average price of $1.50 per unit.

a. What is the money value of output?

b. What is the money income of individuals?

c. Find consumer spending when individuals spend 90 percent of their income.

d. What money revenues are received by the business sector from consumer spending?

e. What is the relationship of the cost of producing output and the money receipts of businesses when there are only consumer expenditures? What should happen to the level of output?

Solution:

a. The money value of output equals the output times the average price per unit. The money value of output is $750 ($500 \times \$1.50$).

b. Since individuals receive an amount equal to the money value of output, their money income is $750.

c. Individuals are spending $675—0.90 times their $750 money income. There is a $75 saving leakage from the circular flow.

d. Business revenues equal the sum of aggregate spending. Since individuals are the only source of spending, revenues equal $675.

e. Businesses are making payments of $750 to produce output, while individuals are purchasing only $675 of what is produced. Because business firms are left holding unsold output valued at $75, they can be expected to decrease output.

Solved Problem 5.2 Suppose there are no gross imports, gross exports, government taxes, or government expenditures for Figure 5-2.

a. What is the equilibrium level of output?

b. What is the level of saving and investment when output is $400, $500, and $600?

c. There being no gross imports or exports, what is the relationship of saving leakages and investment injections when output is above and below the equilibrium output?

Solution:

a. The equilibrium level of output is $500, determined by the point of intersection of the aggregate spending line $(C + I)'$ and the 45° line.

b. Saving at each level of output is the difference between the income received and the amount consumed; in the graph, it is the difference between the consumption line C' and the 45° line. Consumption is $350 and saving is $50 when $Y = \$400$. Saving is $100 when $Y = \$500$, and $150

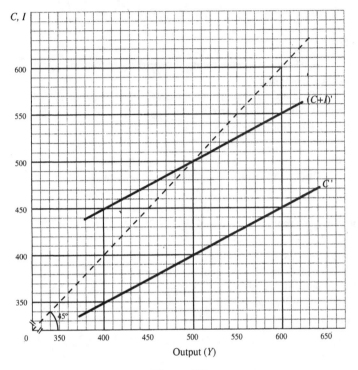

Figure 5-2

when $Y = \$600$. Investment spending is $100, the distance between the consumption line and the aggregate spending line.

c. When output is below the equilibrium level of output, investment injections are greater than saving leakages, e.g., saving is $50 when $Y = \$400$ while $I = \$100$. When output is above the equilibrium level of output, investment injections are smaller than saving leakages, e.g., saving is $150 when $Y = \$600$ while $I = \$100$. At equilibrium, saving leakages equal investment injections.

Solved Problem 5.3

a. Find the value of the multiplier when MPC $= 0.50, 0.75$, and 0.80.

b. Find the relationship between the multiplier and the MPC.

c. Find the change in the equilibrium level of output when there is a $10 increase in net export spending and the MPC $= 0.50, 0.75$, and 0.80.

Solution:

a. When the MPC = 0.50, the value of the multiplier is 2 [$k = 1/(1 - 0.50) = 2$]. The multiplier is 4 when the MPC is 0.75 and 5 when it is 0.80.

b. The value of the multiplier is directly related to the magnitude of MPC, i.e., the greater the MPC, the larger the value of the multiplier.

c. The change in the equilibrium level of output is found by solving the equation $\Delta Y = k(\Delta X_n)$ for ΔY. When MPC = 0.50, the change in the equilibrium level of output is +\$20 [$\Delta Y = 2(\$10) = \$20$]. The change in equilibrium level of output is +\$40 when the MPC = 0.75, and +\$50 when the MPC = 0.80.

Chapter 6
FISCAL POLICY

IN THIS CHAPTER:

✔ *Level of Output with Government Expenditures or Taxes*

✔ *Discretionary Fiscal Policy*

✔ *Built-In Stabilizers*

✔ *Government Deficit and Debt*

✔ *Implementing Fiscal Policy*

✔ *True or False Questions*

✔ *Solved Problems*

Level of Output with Government Expenditures or Taxes

Taxes reduce personal disposable income and therefore consumption and aggregate spending, whereas government expenditures increase aggregate spending. The influence of government expenditures and of taxes upon aggregate spending is shown in Figure 6-1 in the shift of aggregate spending line $(C + I + X_n + G)$. An increase in net lump-sum tax revenues, *ceteris paribus*, shifts the aggregate spending line downward to $(C + I + X_n + G)'$, since higher taxes reduce consumer disposable income and therefore consumer spending at each level of output. An increase in gov-

56

ernment spending, *ceteris paribus*, shifts the aggregate spending line upward to $(C + I + X_n + G)''$. It therefore follows that the government can alter the economy's equilibrium level of output by changing its expenditures or net tax revenues. Such government actions are classified as discretionary fiscal policy.

Discretionary Fiscal Policy

Discretionary fiscal policy involves intentional changes in government spending and/or net tax revenues in order to alter the level of aggregate spending. We have already found that an increase in government spending and/or a decrease in lump-sum taxes shifts the aggregate spending line upward and raises the equilibrium level of output, while a decrease in government spending and/or an increase in lump-sum taxes shifts the aggregate spending line downward and lowers the equilibrium level of output. The government can use discretionary fiscal actions (changing government spending and/or lump-sum taxes) to eliminate an inflationary or recessionary gap.

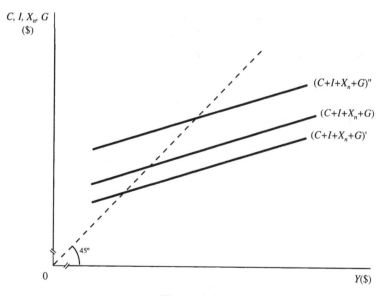

Figure 6-1

Important Things to Remember

In the real world, the government may change its spending and taxing policies for economic reasons or for purely political reasons.

A discretionary fiscal action has a multiplier effect upon the equilibrium level of output. The size of the multiplier depends upon whether there is a change in government spending, or in net lump-sum tax revenues, and there is an income tax. The value for the multiplier for the change in government spending is $\Delta Y/\Delta G$, while the value of the multiplier for the change in net lump-sum tax revenues is $\Delta Y/\Delta T$. When there is no income tax, a change in government spending has the same multiplier effect $[k = 1/(1 - MPC)]$ as does a similar change in investment spending or net exports. The multiplier is smaller for changes in net lump-sum tax revenues; the tax multiplier $k_t = -MPC(k)$ or $-MPC/(1 - MPC)$ is for an economy with no income tax.

An income tax reduces the value of both the expenditure and the lump-sum tax revenue multiplier since the amount of taxes paid to government is directly related to income earned. For example, when the income tax rate is 20 percent and personal income increases \$10, tax payments to the government rise \$2 and personal disposable income increases \$8 rather than \$10. Thus, an increase in  personal income results in smaller increments in induced consumption, and therefore results in a smaller multiplied effect. When there is an income tax, the equation for the expenditure multiplier is $k = 1/[1 - MPC + MPC(t)]$, where t is the income tax rate. The equation for the lump-sum tax multiplier is $k_t = -MPC(k)$ or $-MPC/[1 - MPC + MPC(t)]$.

Built-In Stabilizers

Personal income taxes and various government transfers automatically change the level of net tax revenues when the economy moves away (or toward) the full-employment level of output. For example, government collects smaller revenues from income taxes when output decreases; lump-sum tax revenues also fall when output decreases because of increased government transfer payments to individuals in the form of unemployment insurance benefits, food stamps, and other government assistance programs. Because of such automatic changes in net tax revenues, consumer disposable income is not completely dependent on the level of output, consumer spending is more stable over the business cycle, and the amplitude of economic fluctuations is lessened.

 **Note!**

Built-in stabilizers only help to mitigate economic fluctuations, not to correct them.

Government Deficit and Debt

A federal deficit exists when government outlays exceed revenues. The structural deficit is the deficit that exists when output is at its full-employment level; a cyclical deficit is the amount of the deficit that is attributable to output being below its full-employment level. In Figure 6-2, y_f represents full-employment output. Here the economy's structural deficit is $200 ($500 in government spending less $300 in net tax receipts). Note that the deficit increases to $300 when output declines to y_1, which is not surprising since there are smaller tax receipts and larger government transfers at output levels below y_f. Thus, at output y_1, the $300 deficit consists of a $200 structural deficit and a $100 cyclical deficit.

The public debt is the amount of interest-bearing debt issued by the federal government at a given point in time and arises from previous yearly deficits. Some argue that a large public debt will result in default and federal bankruptcy. The federal government will not default, however, since it has the power to print money and the power to tax. The government can also repay a maturing debt obligation by issuing a new debt obligation. However, due to possible redistribution effects, there is concern about the large increases in the U.S. federal debt. A rapidly rising debt level necessitates larger interest payments. If the government increases

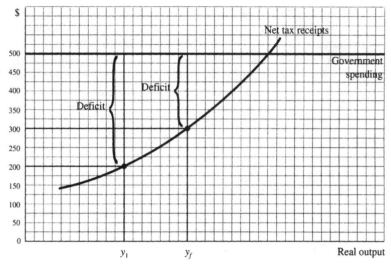

Figure 6-2

taxes to pay its higher interest expense, it could cause a redistribution of income from those who pay taxes to those who have substantial wealth.

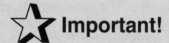

> ## Important!
>
> There is a difference between the deficit and the debt. The former occurs yearly and the latter is an accumulation of the former deficits over time.

Implementing Fiscal Policy

Since discretionary changes in tax revenues and government spending have a multiplier effect upon equilibrium output, it would appear that government has the ability to maintain full-employment output by manipulating its net tax revenues and/or spending. Fiscal policy, however, is not as easily implemented or as successful as first suggested. Suppose a recessionary gap exists. Will Congress and the administration agree on an immediate course of action? In reality, an action lag is likely to occur because of conflicting priorities. For example, some individuals may advocate increased government expenditures on public goods, such as the rebuilding of roads, while others may pre- fer government expenditures on services such as public education. Another group may advocate expanded welfare services or reduced tax rates for middle-income workers. And once a fiscal plan of action is reached and implemented, will Congress and the administration be prepared to scale down or eliminate any of these measures should the fiscal stimulus eventually become excessive?

Besides political priorities, we must also recognize that economic activity exists in a dynamic, changing environment, where other variables may change. Thus, while a fiscal stimulus may close a recessionary gap and bring the economy to full employment, *ceteris paribus*, it is possible that investment and/or net export spending may increase after the fiscal stimulus is implemented, which would result in an inflationary gap. In addition, economists are uncertain about the output level at which full employment exists and have been unable to establish precise values for multipliers for the U.S. economy.

True or False Questions

1. Fiscal policy refers to any change in government tax revenue and/or in government spending.

2. With no income tax and the MPC equal to 0.80, a $10 increase in transfer payments shifts the aggregate spending line upward by $8.

3. With no income tax and the MPC equal to 0.75, a $10 decrease in net tax revenues results in a $30 increase in the equilibrium level of output.

4. When the MPC is 0.75 and the income tax rate is 0.20, the lump-sum multiplier is −3.

5. The availability of food stamps is an example of discretionary fiscal policy.

Answers: 1. True; 2. True; 3. True; 4. False; 5. False

Solved Problems

Solved Problem 6.1 How do the following events affect an aggregate spending line?

a. A $15 increase in government spending.

b. A $10 decrease in investment spending.

c. A $15 decrease in net tax revenues when the MPC is 0.80.

Solution:

a. The aggregate spending line shifts upward by ΔG, the amount of the change in government spending. In this case, there is a corresponding $15 upward shift of the aggregate spending line.

b. Changes in investment shift the aggregate spending line by ΔI. Here, there is a $10 downward shift of the aggregate spending line.

c. Changes in lump-sum taxes shift the aggregate spending line by $-$ MPC(ΔT). Since net tax revenues decrease $15, there is a $12 upward shift of the aggregate spending line [$12 = -0.80(-\$15)$].

Solved Problem 6.2 Suppose there is full employment at the $600 level of output and the MPC is 0.80 in Figure 6-3.

a. Does the aggregate spending line $(C + I + X_n + G)$ depict the existence of an inflationary or recessionary gap?

b. What discretionary fiscal action can government implement to close this gap?

c. What discretionary fiscal action is needed when investment spending decreases $5?

Solution:

a. There is a $60 inflationary gap since the equilibrium level of output is $660 and full-employment output is $600.

b. Government spending should be decreased $12 since the necessary decrease in aggregate spending is $60 and the multiplier is 5 [$\Delta Y = k(\Delta G); -\$60 = 5(\Delta G); \Delta G = -\$12$]. An alternative fiscal action is a $15 increase in lump-sum taxes since the tax multiplier is -4 [$\Delta Y = k_t(\Delta T); -\$60 = -4(\Delta T); \Delta T = +\$15$].

c. The inflationary gap is $35 rather than $60 since the $5 decrease in investment spending lowers aggregate spending $25. To close the smaller inflationary gap, lump-sum taxes need to be increased $8.75, or government expenditures need to be reduced $7.

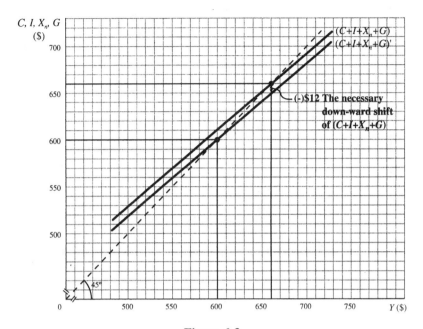

Figure 6-3

Chapter 7

THE FEDERAL RESERVE AND MONETARY POLICY

✔ *Functions of Money*
✔ *Financial Instruments and Markets*
✔ *Creation of M1 Money Supply*
✔ *Federal Reserve System*
✔ *Monetary Tools*
✔ *Open-Market Operations*
✔ *True or False Questions*
✔ *Solved Problems*

Functions of Money

Money serves as a medium of exchange, a measure of value, and a store of value. As a medium of exchange, money is the payment made to economic resources for their services, which the owners of these resources use to purchase goods and services. For example, labor is paid a money

wage; individuals use this money to purchase food
and clothing. Paper currency and checking accounts comprise the medium of exchange in most
countries. Money serves as a measure of value in
that it is the common denominator for measuring
prices and income. For example, a newspaper costs
$0.50 and workers may earn $9.85 per hour. Money functions as a store of value in that the money received today can be saved and held for expenditures at some future date.

Financial Instruments and Markets

Savings can be held in financial assets other than money. Since currency
and checking accounts offer savers little or no interest, many savers are
willing to transfer money balances they do not intend to spend for a period of time into a higher-yielding financial instrument. A credit or debt
financial instrument is one which requires that a borrower make period-
ic interest payments and repay the amount loaned at the end of a contract
period. An equity financial instrument gives the saver partial ownership
of a firm and a share of its profits.

Many financial instruments are marketable and can be sold to another
party in a secondary financial market. A financial instrument is liquid
when the current owner can quickly convert it into a money balance with
a minimal loss of nominal capital value. A saver therefore has a choice of
holding a liquid financial instrument or money as a store of value. The
portfolio decision of holding money, liquid financial instruments, or illiq-
uid financial instruments depends upon the time horizon of the saver, the
return on these alternative instruments, and the willingness of the saver
to assume risk.

You Need to Know ✔

Savers have a host of mediums in which to store
extra money. We mention some major categories
primarily for information purposes.

Depository institutions (commercial banks, savings and loan associations, and credit unions) borrow savers' money balances and lend them to individuals, businesses, or government. By pooling the funds of many small savers and investing in a diversified portfolio of financial instruments, these institutions reduce the transaction costs and risks associated with lending to a borrower. In the U.S., the Federal Deposit Insurance Corporation (FDIC) insures the liabilities of deposit intermediaries. Savers therefore readily hold these liquid liabilities because they normally offer a higher interest return than money. Because the liabilities are liquid and therefore good stores of value, the Federal Reserve presents an M1, M2, and M3 definition of money. The M1 definition is a transaction definition and consists of currency and checking accounts, while M2 and M3 add other liquid financial instruments to the M1 definition.

Current measures of the money supply appear in Table 7.1. Small time deposits are certificates of deposit (CDs) issued by these same financial intermediaries in amounts less than $100,000, and large time deposits exceed this dollar amount. CDs are classified as time deposits since the depositor agrees to keep these funds on deposit for a specified period of time or incur an interest penalty. Repurchase agreements (RPs) are large (at least $1 million) overnight, collateralized loans.

Table 7.1

*M*1		1128.4
Currency outside banks	321.3	
Check-writing deposits	807.1	
*M*2		3564.5
*M*1	1128.4	
Savings deposits plus money-market deposit accounts	1215.5	
Small time deposits	784.7	
Overnight RPs and Eurodollars	86.0	
Noninstitution money-market mutual funds	349.9	
*M*3		4228.3
*M*2	3564.5	
Large time deposits	338.8	
Institution money-market mutual funds	197.0	
Term RPs and Eurodollars	128.0	

Creation of M1 Money Supply

When a bank lends, it gives the borrower a check drawn upon itself. The Federal Reserve controls the banking system's ability to issue check-writing deposits by imposing a reserve requirement on checking deposits. U.S. bank reserves consist of currency held by banks and deposits that banks have at the Federal Reserve. The reserve requirement (r) on check-writing deposits is currently 10 percent ($r = 0.10$); it requires that a bank hold $1 in reserves for each $10 in checking account liability it has. Since U.S. banks are managed to maximize profits, they usually expand loans and issue check-writing deposits when they have more reserves than they are required to hold. Even when a bank has no excess reserves, it can lend and create new checking deposits if it can borrow the excess reserves of other banks.

With banks behaving in this manner, there is a tendency for the excess reserves of the banking system to approximate zero and for the combined sum of check-writing deposits to be a multiple of the amount of reserves held by all banks. When excess reserves for the combined banking system equal zero, the relationship of check-writing deposits (D) and reserves (R) can be presented as $D_{max} = dR$, where d, the check-writing deposit multiplier, equals $1/r$. It therefore follows that the Federal Reserve can control the maximum amount of check-writing deposits by controlling the amount of reserves held by banks and by setting the reserve requirement on checking deposits.

Example 7.1

Suppose the reserve requirement on check-writing deposits is 0.10 and reserves held by all banks total $500,000. The maximum amount of check-writing deposits for the banking system is $5,000,000. $D_{max} = dR$; $d = 1/r$; $d = 1/0.10 = 10$; since $R = $500,000$, $D_{max} = (10)$500,000 = $5,000,000.

 **Note!**

Banks are essential to the U.S. monetary system as the Federal Reserve System can only work through these businesses.

Federal Reserve System

The Federal Reserve System manages the U.S. money supply in order to minimize inflationary pressures and promote economic stability. The Federal Reserve System, frequently referred to as the Fed, consists of twelve Federal Reserve Banks, a Board of Governors, and a Federal Open Market Committee. The Federal Reserve System is considered independent in that its policy directives are not directly influenced by the congressional or executive branches of the federal government.

Federal Reserve Banks. Each of the twelve Federal Banks has its own president, services banks in a specific geographical area, and acts as a central bank for that region. A Federal Reserve Bank clears checks between banks, supervises and regulates banks in its region, performs bank examinations, provides currency to banks, and holds bank reserves. Private individuals and corporations do not deal directly with a Federal Reserve Bank.

Board of Governors. The seven-member Board of Governors is the policy-making body of the Fed. Each member of the Board is nominated by the President of the United States for a fourteen-year, nonrenewable term. Because appointments to the Board are terminal and last for many years, members of the Board of Governors are free of political considerations in the formulation of monetary policy.

Federal Open Market Committee (FOMC). The twelve-member FOMC is responsible for implementing U.S. monetary policy. It establishes directives for open-market operations which determine the M1 money supply. The seven-member Board of Governors and five Federal Reserve Bank presidents comprise the FOMC.

Monetary Tools

The Fed supplies the private sector with whatever amount of currency it wants to hold—thus, the currency component of the M1 money supply is determined by the private sector. Monetary tools available to the Fed include changes in the reserve requirement, open-market operations that control the amount of reserves held by banks, and adjusting the discount rate, which may influence the amount of reserves banks borrow from Federal Reserve Banks.

Reserve-Requirement Variation. A decrease in the reserve requirement on check-writing deposits (monetary ease) creates excess reserves and increases the amount of check-writing deposits issued by banks. Similarly, an increase in the reserve requirement (monetary tightness) decreases the check-writing component of M1. While reserve-requirement variation is a powerful means of changing the M1 money supply, it is used infrequently. Monetary ease or tightness is usually done incrementally. Weekly or monthly changes in the reserve requirement are abrupt and would create management problems for the large number of banks that exist in the U.S.

Open-Market Operations. Open-market operations consist of the purchase and sale of government securities (debt obligations of the U.S. Treasury) by the Fed and are directed by the FOMC. When the Fed purchases government securities, it pays for these bonds by crediting the deposit account banks have at a Federal Reserve Bank. Since reserves include these deposits, such security purchases increase bank reserves and eventually the amount of check-writing deposits issued by banks. Federal Reserve sales of government bonds reduce bank reserves and check-writing deposits, and thereby the M1 money supply.

Discount Rate. A bank may borrow reserves (discount) from a Federal Reserve Bank when it has a reserve deficiency; the rate of interest it pays the Fed is the discount rate. Banks are encouraged to remedy a deficiency by borrowing the excess reserves of other banks in the Fed funds market rather than borrow at the Fed. So, the Fed frequently changes the discount rate after an increase or decrease in the Fed funds rate to encourage this practice. A discount rate change is newsworthy in that it confirms the direction of the movement in the Fed funds rate of interest and interest rates in general.

Important!

Open-market operations are the primary tool of the Fed and are used practically daily to accomplish the Fed's goals.

Open-Market Operations

A change in the M1 money supply affects the short-term rate of interest when there is no change in the private sector's demand for money. There are numerous reasons why the private sector holds money balances. These reasons can be categorized into types of demand, as follows: (1) a transaction demand, since money is needed to purchase goods and services, to pay employees, etc.; (2) a precautionary demand, since money may be held to meet emergency and unforeseen needs that may arise; (3) a portfolio (asset) demand, since some money balances are held in the expectation of opportunities in the financial markets. When there is a fixed demand for money, an increase in the M1 money supply lowers the short-term nominal rate of interest, *ceteris paribus*.

Example 7.2

L' in Figure 7-1 depicts the demand for money. The amount of money demanded is inversely related to the rate of interest since the holder of money forgoes a higher interest return from an alternative financial asset. When the Fed purchases government securities in the open market, bank reserves increase as does the M1 money supply. Thus, money supply curve S' in Figure 7-1 shifts rightward to S'' as the M1 money supply increases and the short-term rate of interest falls from i_0 to i_1.

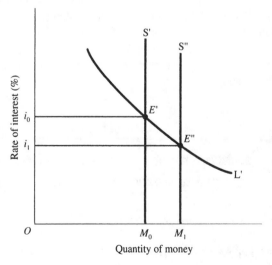

Figure 7-1

The downward pressure on short-term interest rates due to an increase in the money supply is also evident when we consider the effect that an increase in bank reserves has upon bank lending. In purchasing government securities and supplying more reserves to the banking system, the Fed increases the supply of excess reserves. Banks can encourage more borrowers to apply for bank loans by lowering their lending rates. Consumer spending on large-ticketed items such as houses and cars is interest-sensitive since individuals are likely to take out loans to pay for major purchases. Business investment—purchases of new buildings and equipment—is also interest sensitive. Thus, as depicted below, a Fed increase in the money supply should lower the rate of interest, increase interest-sensitive spending, and result in a higher level of spending and gross domestic output.

$$\uparrow M \rightarrow \downarrow i \rightarrow \uparrow \text{ total spending} \rightarrow \uparrow \text{ gross domestic product}$$

True or False Questions

1. A savings deposit is a medium of exchange.
2. A marketable financial instrument can be traded on a secondary market.
3. The banking system's ability to issue check-writing deposits is limited by the reserve requirement on checking deposits and the amount of reserves held by the bank.
4. The maximum increase in check-writing deposits is $100,000, *ceteris paribus*, when the Fed purchases government securities valued at $10,000 and the reserve requirement is 10 percent.
5. When there is a stable demand-for-money curve, a decrease in the M1 money supply lowers the short-term nominal rate of interest.
6. Bank reserves increase and the fed funds rate decreases when the Fed purchases government securities, *ceteris paribus*.

Answers: 1. False; 2. True; 3. True; 4. True; 5. False; 6. True

Solved Problems

Solved Problem 7.1.
a. Why are check-writing deposits included in the definition of money?

b. Is there backing for coins, paper currency, and check-writing deposits?

c. How can money have value without commodity backing?

Solution:

a. In most cases, one can pay for the purchase of a good or service with cash or by writing a check. Since checks are accepted as payment, they are classified as money along with coins and paper currency.

b. In the U.S., coins, paper currency, and checking accounts have no intrinsic value. While coins have a metallic content, the market value of the coined material is considerably less than the face (monetary) value of the coin. Paper currency is issued by the Fed and has no commodity backing, while check-writing deposits are noncollateralized liabilities of deposit institutions.

c. Anything has value when its supply is limited and demand is virtually unlimited. The basis for value for an inconvertible paper standard (coins, paper currency, and checking accounts) is that government can and is willing to limit its supply, economic units are willing to receive it in payment for services, and spending units can use it to obtain goods and services.

Solved Problem 7.2 Why are financial intermediaries essential to the efficient operation of the economy?

Solution: An economic system is judged efficient when it achieves maximum use of economic resources and maximum satisfaction of consumer wants. Financial instruments and institutions generate efficiency in the following ways:

a. The financial system increases consumer satisfaction by facilitating the allocation of spending over time. It allows some units to spend more than their current income (dissave) and allows other spending units to increase their future spending level by earning interest on the money they have saved.

b. The creation of safe and liquid financial claims by financial intermediaries reduces the likelihood that some savers will hold money balances idle. By rechanneling savings into the circular flow, spending flows are stabilized. This in turn stabilizes employment and economic activity.

c. Financial instruments encourage savers to lend their savings to those who want to spend more than their current money inflow. A large portion of the funds borrowed from savers is used by business firms to add to the economy's capital stock. This increases productive capacity.

d. Since the profit motive guides the operation of financial institutions, money saving is distributed to those capital uses that have the greatest productivity.

Solved Problem 7.3 Suppose the banking system holds no excess reserves.

a. What is the maximum amount of check-writing deposits issued by the banking system when reserves total $1,000 and the reserve requirement is (1) 0.20, (2) 0.16, and (3) 0.10?

b. Find the maximum amount of check-writing deposits when the reserve requirement is 0.20 and reserves total (1) $1,000, (2) $1,250, and (3) $2,000.

c. Compare the quantity of check-writing deposits when reserves are held constant and the reserve requirement is lowered in (a) with the quantity of deposits when the amount of reserves held by banks is increased and the reserve requirement remains constant in b.

Solution:

a. The maximum amount of check-writing deposits is found by solving $D_{max} = R/r$. (1) D_{max} is $5,000 ($D_{max} = $1,000/0.20$); (2) $6,250; and (3) $10,000.

b. When the reserve requirement remains at 0.20 and bank reserves increase from $1,000 to $1,250 to $2,000, check-writing deposits increase from (1) $5,000 to (2) $6,250 to (3) $10,000.

c. The situations in a. and b. show that the Fed has two alternative ways of bringing about similar increases in the amount of check-writing deposits; by lowering the reserve requirement or by increasing the amount of reserves held by the banking system.

IN THIS CHAPTER:

✔ *Using Monetary and Fiscal Policy*
✔ *Problems with Fiscal and Monetary Policy*
✔ *Price Level Changes*
✔ *Choosing Fiscal or Monetary Policy*
✔ *True or False Questions*
✔ *Solved Problems*

Using Monetary and Fiscal Policy

Previous chapters have shown that monetary and fiscal policies are alternative ways of changing aggregate spending to close GDP gaps. For example, if output is below its full-employment level, an increase in the money supply, an increase in government spending, or a decrease in taxes raises aggregate spending and increases equilibrium output.

Example 8.1

Suppose the expenditure multiplier k_e is 5, the tax multiplier k_t is –4, and full-employment output exists at $900. If equilibrium output is $800, shifting the aggregate spending line upward can close the $100 recession-

ary gap and bring the economy to full-employment
output. This could be accomplished by a $20 increase
in government spending [$\Delta Y = k_e \Delta G$; $100 = 5($20)],
a $25 decrease in lump-sum taxes, or an increase in
the money supply which lowers interest rates and increases investment spending $20.

Problems with Fiscal and Monetary Policy

An expansionary fiscal policy might not result in an increase in output
exactly equal to $k_e \Delta G$ because of the crowding-out effect. Government
spending increases, which raise the level of output, will usually push the
rate of interest higher. Private-sector interest-sensitive spending will
thereby fall and be crowded out by the fiscal action. Thus, the net increase
in equilibrium output due to increased government spending is usually
less than $k_e \Delta G$. How much less depends upon the interest sensitivity of
the demand for money and the interest sensitivity of investment spending.

Example 8.2

Suppose k_e is 5, full-employment output exists when output is $900, and
equilibrium output is initially $800. A $20 increase in government spending, *ceteris paribus*, should increase spending $100 and bring output to
its full-employment level. But suppose the rate of interest increases as a
result of the $20 increase in government spending and investment spend-
ing declines $5. The net effect of the government's fiscal action is then
$75 rather than $100, and full-employment output is not reached. The net
effect equals $\Delta G(k_e) + \Delta I(k_e) = $20(5) - $5(5) = 75. Since policymak-
ers do not know in advance the extent to which there will be crowding
out, the effect of a stimulative fiscal policy upon output is uncertain.

You Need to Know ✔

Crowding out may partially negate fiscal policies
and so must be considered carefully when implementing any action.

Normally, the rate of interest falls and interest-sensitive spending and equilibrium output increase when the Fed increases the money supply. While most economists agree that changes in the money supply impact interest-sensitive spending, there is substantial disagreement about the predictability of the effect. Keynesians have traditionally argued that there is considerable uncertainty about the effect a money supply change has upon the rate of interest and the level of investment. Monetarists contend that a change in the money supply has a highly predictable effect upon nominal GDP. The disagreement about the predictability of a money supply change has centered around the velocity of money (average circulation of a unit of money in the economy) and its variability. When the demand for money and/or the investment demand are subject to unpredictable shifts, the effect of a money supply change upon equilibrium output is uncertain.

Price Level Changes

In an aggregate demand and aggregate supply framework, an economic stimulus is constrained by a possible increase in the price level. (Note: previous chapters assumed there would be no increase in the price level until the economy reached its full-employment level of output. Such a scenario is unlikely to exist in the real world.) It therefore follows that the effect on output of a monetary or fiscal stim-  ulus depends upon the slope of the aggregate supply curve. A steeply sloped aggregate supply curve has a smaller effect upon output than a relatively flat one. While the actual steepness of the aggregate supply curve is unknown, it is generally believed that aggregate supply is more steeply sloped the closer output is to its full-employment level.

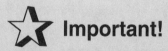 **Important!**

Price level changes constrain any monetary or fiscal policy, but are difficult to counteract because the slopes of the aggregate demand and aggregate supply curves can only be estimated.

Example 8.3

Suppose k_e is 5, there is no crowding out, and full-employment output is $600. Equilibrium output is initially $500 in Figure 8-1 for aggregate demand and aggregate supply curves AD_1 and AS_1. The recessionary gap is $100 since full-employment output is $600; the price level is initially p_0. Since the expenditure multiplier is 5, a $20 increase in government spending should increase output $100 and bring output to its full-employment level when the price level remains at p_0. This $100 increase in spending is presented in Figure 8-1 by the shift of aggregate demand from AD_1 to AD_2. Since aggregate supply AS_1 is positively sloped, the price level rises from p_0 to p_1. This increase in the price level decreases private-sector spending; equilibrium output thus increases to $580 rather than to $600. Suppose the aggregate supply curve is AS_2 rather than AS_1. Figure 8-1 shows that the increase in aggregate demand from AD_1 to AD_2 raises the price level to p_2 rather than p_1, and equilibrium output is $540.

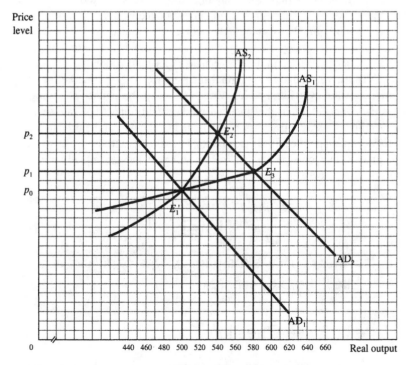

Figure 8-1

Note that there is a smaller increase in equilibrium output but a larger increase in the price level because aggregate supply curve AS_2 is more steeply sloped than AS_1.

Choosing Fiscal or Monetary Policy

Other factors also influence the choice of a monetary or fiscal stimulus: how quickly the economic stimulus impacts economic activity and how the economic stimulus affects the economy's structure of output. A change in government spending normally has the most immediate impact on economic activity since a change immediately affects spending levels. The response to money supply changes is  more likely to lag. While money supply changes immediately impact the rate of interest, the response of interest-sensitive spending to an interest rate change may not be as immediate since many investment projects are not ready to be started when funding costs decrease. A money supply change, however, has a short action lag since the Fed, unlike Congress, can respond quickly to changing economic conditions. Thus, in spite of its longer impact lag, monetary policy is the principal economic stabilization measure used in the US because of its short action lag.

Those who advocate minimal interference with the market prefer monetary policy to fiscal policy. Monetary policy, through its interest rate effect, works through the financial markets and impacts private-sector spending; a fiscal action may redistribute income within the private sector or expand public rather than private-sector goods and services. For example, a change in the personal income tax rate does not equally impact each income class.

★ Note!

Monetary policy is the primary type of policy used to affect the U.S. economy.

True or False Questions

1. An increase in government spending always crowds out an equal amount of private-sector interest-sensitive spending.

2. The net increase in equilibrium output is $10 when k_e is 5, government spending increases $10, and higher interest rates crowd out $8 of investment spending.

3. An increase in aggregate demand has no effect upon real output when aggregate supply is vertical.

4. A $10 increase in the money supply increases equilbrium output $50 when k_e is 5, there is no crowding out, and aggregate supply is positively sloped.

5. Monetary policy is more frequently used than fiscal policy since it more quickly impacts aggregate spending.

Answers: 1. False; 2. True; 3. True; 4. False; 5. False

Solved Problems

Solved Problem 8.1 What happens to equilibrium output and the price level in Figure 8-2 when an increase in the money supply shifts aggregate demand from AD_1 to AD_2?

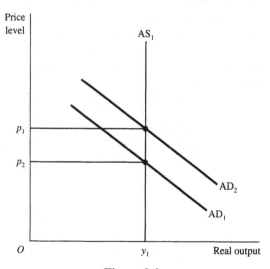

Figure 8-2

Solution: The rightward shift of aggregate demand, caused by an increase in the money supply, has no effect upon equilibrium output but increases the price level from p_2 to p_1. Aggregate demand shifts have no effect upon output whenever the aggregate supply curve is vertical; demand shifts in such an economic situation only affect the price level.

Solved Problem 8.2

a. A stimulative monetary or fiscal action should increase aggregate demand. What factors may limit the actual increase in aggregate demand?

b. An increase in aggregate demand should raise equilibrium output. What is responsible for the size of the increase in equilibrium output?

Solution:

a. Factors that constrain the aggregate demand shift when there is a fiscal or monetary stimulus are crowding out and the interest sensitivity of the demand for money and investment spending. An increase in government spending and/or a decrease in taxes raises output, usually resulting in an increase in the rate of interest. Higher interest rates can crowd out private-sector interest-sensitive investment spending. So, the actual increase in aggregate demand due to a fiscal stimulus depends upon the magnitude of the crowding-out effect. An increase in money supply raises private-sector spending by lowering the rate of interest. The actual decrease in the interest rate depends upon the interest sensitivity of the demand for money. The effect that a decrease in the interest rate has upon spending in turn depends upon the interest sensitivity of investment spending. Thus, a money supply increase can cause a large or small shift of the aggregate demand.

b. An increase in aggregate demand should raise equilibrium output; the actual increase in output depends upon the slope of the aggregate supply curve. When aggregate supply is steeply sloped, demand increases have a smaller effect upon output than when aggregate supply is less steeply sloped.

Chapter 9
ECONOMIC GROWTH AND PRODUCTIVITY

IN THIS CHAPTER:

✔ *Concept of Economic Growth*
✔ *Growth through Population and Capital Accumulation*
✔ *Supply-Side Economics*
✔ *True or False Questions*
✔ *Solved Problems*

Concept of Economic Growth

Economic growth is concerned with the expansion of an economy's ability to produce (potential GDP) over time. Expansion of potential output occurs when there is an increase in natural resources, human resources, or capital, or when there is a technological advance. The two most common measures of economic growth are an increase in real GDP and an increase in output per capita. Of these two measures, an increase in output per capita is more meaningful since it indicates there are more goods and services available per person and hence a rise in the economy's standard of living. An increase in potential output can be conceptualized by an outward shift of an economy's production-possibility frontier. In our discussion of economic growth, we assume that increases in potential output are matched by equal increases in aggregate spending so that full-employment growth is assured.

Growth through Population and Capital Accumulation

An increase in the labor supply, *ceteris paribus*, expands potential output. The law of diminishing returns shows that the incremental output from an additional labor input decreases when other economic resources and technology are unchanged. Thus, the possibility exists that aggregate output could increase while output per capita decreases. Expecting rapid population growth, economists in the early nineteenth century predicted such growth would result in declining output per capita. Thomas Malthus, in particular, held that the population would increase at such a rapid rate that the economy would increasingly be unable to grow enough food to feed its population; eventually output per capita would fall to a subsistence level. While technology has allowed highly industrialized countries to avoid these gloomy projections, rapid population growth is a problem for many developing countries.

Note!

Such theories as that of Thomas Malthus have helped to label economics as the dismal science.

The neoclassical model of economic growth maintains that, in the absence of technological change, an economy reaches a steady state—where there are no further increases in output per capita. In the steady state, capital deepening ceases, although capital widening can occur because of growth in the labor supply. Capital widening exists when capital is added to keep the ratio of capital per worker constant due to increases in the supply of labor. Capital deepening occurs when there is an increase in the ratio of capital to labor.

With no technological advance, capital additions that are capital widening do not change output per worker; however, capital additions that are capital deepening increase output per worker. When there is no change in the labor force, capital additions result in diminishing returns and have decreased rates of return. Capital additions cease—and the economy reaches a steady state—when the rate of return from capital additions equals the economy's real rate of  interest. Since there is a limit to capital deepening when there is no change in technology, there must also be a limit to output per worker and therefore to the economy's standard of living. An economy's steady-state position can be pushed to a higher level of output per worker by an increase in its rate of saving, by improved technology, and/or by better education of its population.

Productivity is measured by dividing real GDP by the total number of hours worked by labor. Over time, the growth of labor productivity in the U.S. has slowed. Economists have been unable to empirically establish the cause of this productivity growth slowdown, but some potential factors may be: (1) an increase in environmental regulations; (2) high energy costs, resulting in the substitution of more labor and capital for energy; and (3) an increase in the number of less skilled workers in the labor force.

A productivity growth slowdown has implications for a country's standard of living. Standard of living is measured by an economy's real GDP per capita (total output divided by population), whereas productivity is measured as real GDP per hour of labor input (output divided by the number of hours worked to produce this output). Suppose an economy's labor force is always 50 percent of its population. Increases in labor's output per hour will result in higher GDP per capita and therefore raise the economy's standard of living. When output per hour is unchanged, there will be no increase in output per capita and therefore no improvement in the economy's standard of living.

Important!

Increased productivity has been the major source of growth for many countries during certain periods, including the U.S.

Supply-Side Economics

Concern about the slowdown in U.S. productivity growth during the 1970s helped popularize the theory of supply-side economics. Supply-siders stressed that U.S. productivity would be enhanced by actions that promoted incentives to produce. A decrease in private-sector taxes was proposed. Proponents of this theory called for a decrease in corporate income tax rates, which would increase corporate profits and therefore business saving. This in turn would encourage business investment and capital accumulation. A reduction in the personal income tax rate would increase the reward from working, which might increase labor productivity. Decreased tax rates on interest income and corporate dividends would increase household saving, which would result in capital deepening. While not identified as supply-side economics, various measures were promoted in the 1990s that would also increase the economy's ability to produce. Improvement of the U.S. educational system would enhance labor skills, increase labor productivity, and thereby promote economic growth.

You Need to Know

Supply-siders can come from any political party, but different groups tend to favor specific policies (i.e., tax cuts or increased education).

Example 9.1

In Figure 9-1, assume that the labor supply and population are unchanged and that a combination of tax incentives and a better-educated population shift the aggregate supply curve AS_1 to AS_2. An increase in the money supply shifts aggregate demand from AD_1 to AD_2; the price level remains constant and output increases from y_1 to y_2. Since there is no change in population, output per capita has increased with an attending rise in the economy's standard of living.

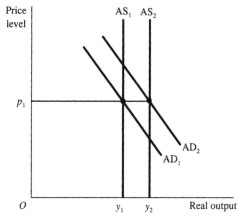

Figure 9-1

True or False Questions

1. An economy's standard of living is rising when real GDP is increasing 10 percent while population is increasing 5 percent.

2. Assuming full employment of resources, an increase in the labor force, *ceteris paribus*, always increases output per capita.

3. Additions to the economy's stock of capital always result in capital deepening and capital widening.

4. Supply-side policies intend to increase the economy's ability to produce.

5. The slowdown in U.S. productivity growth was caused by capital widening.

Answers: 1. True; 2. False; 3. False; 4. True; 5. False

Solved Problems

Solved Problem 9.1 Table 9.1 presents growth in real GDP for Country A and Country B. For each country find:
   a. Relative increase in output between 1984 and 1994.
   b. Output per capita for 1984 and 1994.

Table 9.1

	1984	1994
Country A		
Real GDP	$650,000,000	$1,300,000,000
Population	166,000	224,000
Country B		
Real GDP	$528,614,000	$1,295,100,000
Population	135,000	270,000

c. Relative increase in output per capita between 1984 and 1994.

d. Which measure of economic growth, as calculated in a. or c., is more useful?

Solution:

a. The relative increase in output is found by dividing 1994 GDP by that for 1984. The relative increase in Country A's real GDP is 2.0; thus, Country A's real GDP doubled between 1984 and 1994. The relative increase for Country B is 2.45 for the same period.

b. An economy's per capita GDP is found by dividing real GDP by the economy's population. In Country A, per capita output is $3,915.66 in 1984 and $5,803.57 in 1994. Country B's per capita output increased from $3,915.66 in 1984 to $4,796.67 in 1994.

c. The relative increase in per capita output between 1984 and 1994 is found by dividing per capita output in 1994 by that in 1984. The relative increase in per capita output is 1.48 for Country A and 1.22 for Country B.

d. Economic growth is frequently presented as the increase in real GDP. While useful for some analysis, increases in real GDP do not measure the economic well-being of individuals in an economy, which is best measured by increases in per capita output. The calculations in parts a. and c. show how one might reach different conclusions about an economy's economic growth. Country B's real GDP more than doubled between 1984 and 1994, while A's only doubled; B obviously has increased its output at a faster rate than A. On a per capita basis, however, output per capita increased more rapidly in Country A than B. Which measure is more useful depends upon one's intent in measuring growth. When one is only interested in the increase in aggregate output, growth in real GDP is the relevant measure. However, when the focus is upon the standard of living in the economy, output per capita is the better measure of economic growth.

Solved Problem 9.2 What objections, if any, are there to economic growth?

Solution: Some economists object to maximizing economic growth because in doing so it may possibly affect the quality of life, in such ways as pollution of the environment or waste of natural resources. Maximized economic growth may also fail to resolve socioeconomic problems or may exacerbate them. Rapid economic growth through technological change in many instances increases worker obsolescence (workers no longer have skills needed in the labor market), brings about new anxieties and insecurities, and undermines family relationships as the workplace takes on greater importance than human relationships. Although attempts are being made to curb pollution, industrial waste is a by-product of increased output. It therefore can be expected that water, land, and air pollution will increase with time. Waste of economic resources may also result when least-cost methods dictate current resource use with little attention paid to the possible effect that current use may have upon future generations. And there is no guarantee that growth resolves socioeconomic problems such as poverty. Poverty in an economy is relative to the economy's standard of living. Thus, growth does not resolve the problem of relative poverty, which is only resolved by a redistribution of current income.

Chapter 10
INTERNATIONAL TRADE AND FINANCE

IN THIS CHAPTER:

- ✔ *Basis of and Gains from Trade*
- ✔ *Obstacles to Trade*
- ✔ *Balance of Payments*
- ✔ *Exchange Rates*
- ✔ *True or False Questions*
- ✔ *Solved Problems*

Basis of and Gains from Trade

Thus far, we have assumed a relatively closed economy, or an economy isolated from the rest of the world. In reality, most nations are open economies. That is, they are connected to other nations through a network of trade and financial relationships. These relationships have great advantages but they may also result in problems. Even though trade is generally more important to small than to large developed  nations, the welfare of the latter is also greatly dependent on trade.

Since the availability of resources differs among nations, the opportunity cost of producing more of a commodity (in terms of the amount of another commodity that would not be produced) also usually differs among nations. In a two-nation, two-commodity world, each nation should specialize in the production of the commodity with the lower opportunity cost; this is the commodity in which the nation has a comparative advantage. The nation should trade part of its output with the other nation for the commodity with the higher opportunity cost (the one in which the nation has a comparative disadvantage). This leads to a larger combined output of both commodities than would occur in the absence of specialization and trade.

 **Note!**

Comparative advantage is the key to trade among countries.

Example 10.1

Figure 10-1 shows a hypothetical production-possibilities frontier for cloth (C) and food (F) for the U.S. and U.K. under constant costs (the solid lines).

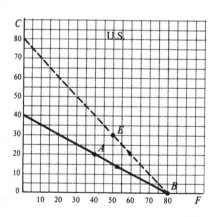 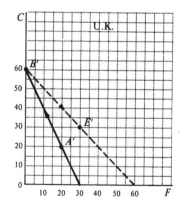

Figure 10-1

It shows that the U.S. could produce alternatives including 40C and 0F, or 0C and 80F. For each unit of cloth the U.S. gives up, it releases resources to produce two additional units of food. The domestic cost ratio is 1C = 2F, or 1/2C = 1F, and is constant in the U.S. In the U.K., 2C = 1F. Since the opportunity cost of F is 1/2C in the U.S. and 2C in the U.K., the U.S. has a comparative advantage in F. Similarly, the U.K. has a comparative advantage in C. Suppose that in the absence of trade, the U.S. and U.K. produced and consumed at points A (20C and 40F) and A' (20C and 20F), respectively. With trade, the U.S. should specialize in the production of F and produce at B (80F and 0C) and the U.K. should specialize in C and produce at B' (60C and 0F). By then exchanging, say, 30F for 30C with the U.K., the U.S. would end up consuming at E (30C and 50F) and the U.K. would consume at E' (30C and 30F). Thus, both the U.S. and the U.K. end up consuming 10C and 10F more than without specialization and trade (compare E with A and E' with A'). With increasing opportunity costs, the production-possibilities frontiers are concave or bulge outward, and there would be incomplete specialization in production.

Obstacles to Trade

Even though trade can be the source of major gains, most nations restrict the free flow of trade by imposing tariffs, quotas, and other obstructions. An *import tariff* is a tax on the imported commodity. An *import quota* is a quantitative restriction on the amount of a good that may be imported during a year. Other restrictions include health regulations and safety and pollution standards. Trade restrictions are advocated by labor and firms in some industries as a protection against foreign competition. These restrictions, however, generally impose a burden on society as a whole because they reduce the availability of goods and increase their prices. Some of the specific arguments advanced for trade restrictions are: (1) to protect domestic labor against cheap foreign labor; (2) to reduce domestic unemployment; (3) to protect young or "infant" industries; and (4) to protect industries important for national defense. Most of the arguments are invalid and are based on misconceptions.

You Need to Know ✔

Trade restrictions are often supported by groups that will specifically benefit from the restrictions, oftentimes at the expense of other groups.

Balance of Payments

The balance of payments is a yearly summary statement of a nation's transactions with the rest of the world. The balance of payments is divided into three major sections: (1) current account, which shows flows of good and services and government grants; (2) capital account, which shows flows of investments and loans; and (3) official reserve account, which shows the change in the nation's official government reserves and liabilities to balance the current and capital accounts.

The nation gains foreign currencies by exporting goods and services and receiving capital inflows (i.e., investments and loans) from abroad; all of these are credits. The nation spends these foreign currencies to import goods and services and to invest and lend abroad; these are debits. When the sum of all these debits exceeds the sum of the credits in the current and capital accounts, the nation has a deficit in its balance of payments equal to the difference. The deficit is settled by a reduction in the nation's reserves of foreign currency or by an increase in the foreign country's holdings of the deficit nation's currency. The opposite is true for a balance-of-payments surplus.

Exchange Rates

A nation generates a supply of foreign currencies or monies in the process of exporting goods and services and receiving grants, investments, and loans from abroad. On the other hand, the nation uses foreign currencies to import goods and services and to make grants, investments, and loans abroad. When foreign currencies can be freely bought and sold, the rate of exchange between the domestic and a foreign currency is determined by the market demand for and the supply of the foreign currency. If the demand for the foreign currency increases, the rate of exchange rises. That is, more domestic currency is required to purchase one unit of the foreign currency (so that the domestic currency depreciates).

Example 10.2

In Figure 10-2, D is the U.S. demand and S is the U.S. supply curve for pounds (£, the currency of the U.K.).

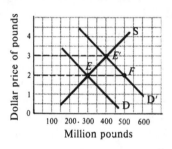

Figure 10-2

D is downward sloping because at lower dollar prices for pounds it is cheaper for the U.S. to import from, invest in, and extend loans to the U.K. S is upward sloping because at higher dollar prices for pounds, it is cheaper for the U.K. to import from, invest in, and extend loans to the U.S. D and S intersect at the equilibrium rate of exchange of $2 = £1 and the equilibrium quantity of £300 million. If D shifts up to D′, the rate of exchange rises to $3 = £1. If, on the other hand, the rate of exchange is not allowed to rise (as under the fixed-exchange system), the U.S. would have a deficit with the U.K. of EF = £200 = $400 million in its balance of payments. This deficit could only be corrected by reducing the level of national income, by allowing domestic prices to rise less than abroad, or by government control of trade and payments.

 **Note!**

Foreign currencies have prices (i.e., exchange rates), just like any other good or service.

From the end of World War II until 1971, the world operated under a fixed-exchange-rate system known as the Bretton Woods System. Under this system, the U.S. faced large and chronic deficits, which it was justifiably unwilling to correct by domestic deflation or direct controls on trade and payments. The resulting lack of adjustment forced the abandonment of the fixed-exchange-rate system and the establishment of a flexible-exchange-rate system. However, the system that is in operation today is not freely flexible or completely floating because national monetary authorities intervene in foreign exchange markets to prevent erratic and unwanted fluctuations in exchange rates.

True or False Questions

1. Large countries are generally more open than small countries.
2. When each nation specializes in the production of the commodity of its comparative advantage, the combined output of both commodities increases.
3. Import restrictions are required to protect the nation's labor against foreign competition.
4. A nation has a surplus in its balance of payments if its total credits exceed its total debits in its current and capital accounts.
5. A deficit in a nation's balance of payments is corrected by a depreciation of its currency under a fixed-exchange-rate system.

Answers: 1. True; 2. True; 3. False; 4. True; 5. False

Solved Problems

Solved Problem 10.1

a. How can we measure a nation's degree of economic interdependence with the rest of the world?

b. Why does the U.S. rely less on trade than most other developed nations?

c. What would happen to its standard of living if the U.S. withdrew completely from international trade?

Solution:

a. A rough measure of the degree of interdependence of a nation with the rest of the world is given by the value of its exports as a percentage of its GDP.

b. The U.S. is a nation of continental size with immense natural and human resources. As such, it can produce with relative efficiency most of the products it needs. In contrast, a small nation can only specialize in the production and export of a small range of commodities and must import all the others. In general, the larger the nation, the smaller its economic interdependence with the rest of the world.

c. Even though the U.S. relies only to a relatively small extent on foreign trade, a significant part of its high standard of living depends on it. For one thing, the U.S. is incapable of producing such commodities as coffee, tea, and Scotch whiskey. In addition, the U.S. has no known deposits of such minerals as tin and tungsten, which are important for industrial production. It also needs to import huge quantities of petroleum. In addition, there are many commodities that the U.S. could produce domestically but only at a relatively higher cost than the costs of some foreign countries. Thus, trade is very important to the welfare of the U.S.

Solved Problem 10.2

a. Cite some of the specific arguments advanced in favor of trade protection.

b. Evaluate these arguments.

Solution:

a. Protection is often advocated to protect domestic labor against cheap foreign labor. That is, since wages are generally higher in the U.S. than in other nations, without protection foreign nations can undersell the U.S. because of the lower wages. Another argument for protection is that it reduces domestic unemployment. By restricting imports, domestic production is stimulated and unemployment is reduced. A third argument in favor of protection is the "infant industry" argument. This states that a newly established industry requires protection until it can grow in size and efficiency so as to be able to face foreign competition. Finally, protection is advocated in order to protect such industries as shipyards that are important for national defense.

b. The argument for protection against cheap foreign labor is generally invalid because it incorrectly implies that higher wages necessarily mean higher labor costs. This is not true if the higher U.S. wages are based on even higher labor productivity. Restrictions on U.S. imports to reduce U.S. unemployment is a beggar-thy-neighbor policy because it leads to higher unemployment in those nations whose exports to the U.S. have been restricted. As a result, these other nations can retaliate and also reduce imports from the U.S., and all nations lose in the end. The infant-industry argument is generally invalid for the U.S. and other industrial nations but may be valid for poor developing nations. However, the same degree of protection can generally be better achieved by subsidies to the infant industry rather than by tariffs and quotas. Subsidies are also generally preferable to tariffs and quotas as protection to industries important for national defense.

Solved Problem 10.3

a. What happens to the equilibrium rate of exchange and to the equilibrium quantity of foreign exchange if the nation's demand for the foreign currency decreases? Why?

b. How is a deficit or a surplus in a nation's balance of payments corrected under a flexible-exchange-rate system?

Solution:

a. Given the nation's supply curve of the foreign currency, a downward shift in the nation's demand curve for the foreign currency will determine a new and lower equilibrium exchange rate and equilibrium quantity. A decrease in the nation's demand for a foreign currency may result from a change in tastes for less imported goods and services. It may also occur if the nation decreases its investments and loans abroad in the expectation of decreased returns.

b. A deficit in a nation's balance of payments means that at a given rate of exchange, there is a shortage (an excess of quantity demanded over quantity supplied) of the foreign currency. If the exchange rate is freely flexible or floating, the exchange rate will rise until the quantity demanded of the foreign currency equals the quantity supplied and the deficit is completely eliminated. This rise in the exchange rate means that the relative value of the domestic currency is falling or depreciating. The exact opposite occurs when there is a surplus and the nation's currency appreciates (or increases) in relative value.

Chapter 11

THEORY OF CONSUMER DEMAND AND UTILITY

IN THIS CHAPTER:

- ✔ *Law of Diminishing Marginal Utility*
- ✔ *Utility Maximization*
- ✔ *Derivation of Individual Demand Curve*
- ✔ *True or False Questions*
- ✔ *Solved Problems*

Law of Diminishing Marginal Utility

In previous chapters, we saw that the market demand curve for a commodity is derived by adding the individual's demand curves for the commodity. We also saw that each individual's (and thus the market) demand curve for a commodity is downward-sloping because of the substitution and income effects.

However, an individual demands a particular commodity because of the satisfaction, or utility, he or she receives from consuming it. The more units of a commodity the individual consumes per unit of time, the greater is the total utility he receives. Although total utility increases, the extra, or marginal, utility received from consuming each additional unit of the commodity decreases. This is referred to as the *law of diminishing marginal utility*.

Example 11.1

For purposes of illustration, we assume in Table 11.1 that satisfaction can actually be measured in terms of units of utility called utils. The first two columns of Table 11.1 give an individual's hypothetical total utility (TU) schedule from consuming various quantities of commodity X (say oranges) per unit of time.

Table 11.1

(1) q_x	(2) TU_x	(3) MU_x
0	0	
		10
1	10	
		8
2	18	
		6
3	24	
		4
4	28	
		2
5	30	

Note that as the individual consumes more units of X, TU_x increases. Columns 1 and 3 of the table give this individual's marginal utility (MU) schedule for commodity X. Each value of column 3 is obtained by subtracting two successive values of column 2. For example, if the individual's consumption of X rises from 1 unit to 2 units, TU_x rises from 10 to 18, and the MU of the second unit of X is 8.

Remember

Utility models can be used to predict how consumers will act even if the consumers do not specifically think in terms of units of utility.

Utility Maximization

A consumer maximizes the total utility or satisfaction obtained from spending his income and is in equilibrium when the marginal utility of the last dollar spent on each commodity is the same. This equilibrium condition for utility maximization can be restated as follows:

$$\frac{MU_x}{P_x} = \frac{MU_y}{P_y} = ... = \text{common MU of last \$ spent on each commodity}$$

Example 11.2

Table 11.2 shows the marginal utility that an individual receives from consuming various units of X and Y per unit of time. Suppose that the consumer has \$7 to spend on X and Y, and that P_x (the price of X) = \$2 and P_y = \$1. This consumer maximizes total utility and is in equilibrium by spending \$4 of his \$7 to buy $2X$ and the remaining \$3 to purchase $3Y$. At this point, $MU_x / P_x = 8$ utils / \$2 = $MU_y / P_y = 4$ utils / \$1 = MU of 4 utils from the last \$ spent on X and Y. By purchasing $2X$ and $3Y$, $TU_x = 18$ (from $10 + 8$), $TU_y = 15$ (from $6 + 5 + 4$), and TU from both is 33 utils.

Table 11.2

Units of Commodities	MU_x	MU_y
1	10	6
2	8	5
3	6	4
4	4	3
5	2	2

Derivation of Individual Demand Curve

Starting with an equilibrium, we get one point on a consumer's demand curve. At a lower commodity price, the consumer must purchase more of the commodity to be in equilibrium, and so we can get another point on that demand curve. From these and other points of consumer equilibri-

☆ Note!

Utility maximization theory gives a formula to help explain the shape of the individual demand curve.

um, we can derive a downward sloping demand curve because of diminishing MU. Because MU declines, the price must fall to induce the individual consumer to buy more of the commodity.

Consumer's surplus refers to the difference between what the consumer would be willing to pay to purchase a given number of units of a commodity and what he actually pays for them. It arises because the consumer pays for all units of the commodity the price he is just willing to pay for the last unit purchased, even though the MU on earlier units is greater. Consumer surplus can be measured by the area under the consumer's demand curve and above the commodity price.

You Need to Know

Consumer surplus arises from the different prices consumers would be willing to pay for different quantities of the same good. Imagine how much you would be willing to pay for your first phone call each month, as opposed to your fiftieth call.

Example 11.3

In Figure 11-1, the consumer purchases *AF* units of the commodity at price *AB* and spends *AB* times *AF* (the area of the rectangle *ABCF*) on this commodity. However, this consumer would have been willing to pay a higher price for all but the last unit of this commodity purchased (as indicated by the height of her demand curve) because these previous units give her a greater MU than the last unit purchased. The difference be-

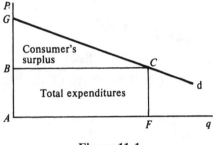

Figure 11-1

tween what she would be willing to pay for *AF* units of the commodity (the area of *AGCF*) and what she actually pays for them (the area of *ABCF*) is an estimate of this consumer's surplus (the area of triangle *BGC*).

True or False Questions

1. The demand curve is downward sloping because of the substitution and income effects.
2. The more of a commodity is consumed, the higher is the total utility derived.
3. The law of diminishing marginal utility states that each successive unit of the commodity consumed leads to a larger addition to total utility.
4. Consumer utility maximization is satisfied by the condition that $MU_x = MU_y = MU_z$.
5. Consumer's surplus can be measured by the area under the demand curve and below the commodity price.

Answers: 1. True; 2. True; 3. False; 4. False; 5. False

Solved Problems

Solved Problem 11.1 Suppose that a consumer has the MU_x and MU_y of Table 11.3, money income of $10, $P_x = \$2$, and $P_y = \$1$.
   a. Describe how this consumer should spend each dollar of her $10

Table 11.3

Units	1	2	3	4	5	6	7	8	9	10
MU_x	14	(12)	11	10	9	8	6	4	3	1
MU_y	13	11	10	8	7	(6)	3	2	0	−5

to purchase each unit of X and Y so as to maximize her total utility or satisfaction.

    b. Show that her TU would be less if she bought one more unit of either X or Y.

    c. Show that the equilibrium condition for utility maximization is satisfied when the consumer purchases 2X and 6Y.

Solution:

    a. Because $P_x = \$2$, if this consumer spent her first $2 to buy the first unit of X, she would receive a MU_x of only 14, or 7 utils per dollar spent on X. On the other hand, if this consumer spent her first dollar to purchase the first unit of Y, she would receive a MU_y of 13, or 13 utils per dollar. Thus, she should spend her first dollar to purchase the first unit of Y and receive 13 utils of satisfaction. Similarly, this consumer should spend her second, third, and fourth dollars to purchase the second, third, and fourth units of Y and receive 11, 10, and 8 utils, respectively. This consumer is indifferent between purchasing the fifth unit of Y or the first unit of X because she receives 7 utils *per dollar* spent on each. She would purchase both and spend her fifth, sixth, and seventh dollars to purchase the fifth Y and the first X (remember, $P_x = \$2$). Similarly, the consumer should spend her eighth, ninth, and tenth (or last) dollar to purchase the sixth Y (and receive 6 utils) and the second X (and receive 12 utils, or 6 utils per dollar). By purchasing 2X and 6Y, this consumer is receiving 81 utils (14 + 12 from X and 13 + 11 + 10 + 8 + 7 + 6 from Y). This is the maximum TU she can receive by spending her total income of $10 on X and Y when $P_x = \$2$ and $P_y = \$1$. Thus, the consumer is in equilibrium by purchasing 2X and 6Y.

    b. To buy the third unit of X (at $P_x = \$2$), this consumer would have to give up the fifth and sixth units of Y (at $P_y = \$1$). She would gain 11 utils by purchasing the third unit of X but lose 13 utils (7 + 6) by giving up her fifth and sixth Y, with a net loss of 2 utils. The consumer's TU would be only 79 utils if she purchased 3X and 4Y (compared with a TU of 81 utils with $2X$ and $6Y$) and she would not be maximizing the TU from spending her $10 of income. On the other hand, by giving up her second X (thus losing 12 utils), this consumer could purchase her seventh and eighth Y (gaining only a total of 5 utils), with a net loss of 7 utils. Purchasing $1X$ and $8Y$, this consumer would receive a total of 74 utils $(81 - 7)$ and would not be in equilibrium.

c. With $2X$ and $6Y$, the consumer is in equilibrium because $MU_x / P_x = 12$ utils $/ \$2 = MU_y / P_y = 6$ utils $/ \$1 = MU$ of 6 utils from the last dollar spent on X and Y. Plus, the consumer's income is exhausted.

Solved Problem 11.2 Why is water, which is essential to life, so cheap, while diamonds, which are not essential to life, so expensive?

Solution: Because water is essential to life, the TU received from water exceeds the TU received from diamonds. However, the price we are willing to pay for each unit of a commodity depends not on the TU but on the MU. We consume so much water that the MU of the last unit of water consumed is very low. Therefore, we are willing to pay only a very low price for the last unit of water consumed. Since all units of water consumed are identical we pay the same low price on all other units of water consumed.

On the other hand, we purchase so few diamonds that the MU of the last diamond purchased is very high. Therefore, we are willing to pay a high price for this last diamond and for all the other diamonds purchased.

Solved Problem 11.3 With MU_x and MU_y of Table 11.3, income of $10, $P_x = \$2$, and $P_y = \$1$, the consumer is in equilibrium by purchasing $2X$ and $6Y$ (see Solved Problem 11.1)

a. Find the point of consumer equilbrium with $P_x = \$1$.

b. How is this consumer's demand schedule for commodity X derived?

Solution:

a. If P_x fall to $1, the consumer will no longer be in equilibrium by continuing to purchase $2X$ and $6Y$ because

$$\frac{MU_x \text{ of } 12 \text{ utils}}{P_x \text{ of } \$1} > \frac{MU_y \text{ of } 6 \text{ utils}}{P_y \text{ of } \$1}$$

and she is spending only $8 of her $10 income. Since the second dollar spent to purchase the second unit of X (at $P_x = \$1$) gives this individual more (marginal) utility than the sixth dollar spent to purchase the sixth unit of Y, the individual should spend more on X and less on Y. As she buys more X, the consumer moves down her diminishing MU_x schedule. As she buys less of Y, she moves up her diminishing MU_y. The consumer will be in equilibrium when the MU of the last dollar spent on X equals the MU of the last dollar spent on Y. This occurs when this consumer spends her $10 to purchase $6X$ and $4Y$ because

$$\frac{MU_x \text{ of 8 utils}}{P_x \text{ of } \$1} > \frac{MU_y \text{ of 8 utils}}{P_y \text{ of } \$1}$$

b. When $P_x = \$2$, this consumer purchases $2X$ in order to be in equilibrium. This gives one point of this demand schedule for commodity X. Other points on the consumer's demand schedule for X can be similarly obtained by allowing P_x to change again and recording q_x at equilibrium (as done in part a.).

Chapter 12
PRODUCTION COSTS

In This Chapter:

- ✔ *Explicit and Implicit Costs*
- ✔ *Short-Run Costs*
- ✔ *Long-Run Costs*
- ✔ *True or False Questions*
- ✔ *Solved Problems*

Explicit and Implicit Costs

In this chapter we concentrate on the firm's production costs—or what lies behind its supply curve. *Explicit costs* are the actual, out-of-pocket expenditures of the firm to purchase the services of the factors of production it needs. *Implicit costs* are the costs of the factors owned by the firm and used in its own production processes. These costs should be estimated from what these factors could earn in their  best alternative use or employment. In economics, costs include both explicit and implicit costs. Profit is the excess of revenues over these costs.

Example 12.1

The explicit costs of a firm are the wages it must pay to hire labor, the interest to borrow money capital, and the rent on land and buildings used in the production process. To these, the firm must add such implicit costs as the wage that the entrepreneur would earn working as a manager for somebody else, the interest he would get by supplying his money capital (if any) to someone else in a similarly risky business, and the rent on his own land and buildings, if he were not using them himself. Only if the total revenue received from selling the output exceeds both its explicit and implicit costs is the firm making an economic or pure profit.

Don't Forget

Both explicit and implicit costs must be considered any time we are considering the true economic costs of a project.

The law of diminishing returns is one of the most important and unchallenged laws of production. This law states that as we get more and more units of a factor of production to work with one or more fixed factors, after a point we get less and less extra or marginal output from each additional unit of the variable factor used. The time period when at least one factor of production is fixed in quantity (i.e., cannot be varied) is referred to as the *short run*. Thus, the law of diminishing returns is a short-run law. In the long run, all factors are variable.

Short-Run Costs

In the short run, there are total fixed costs, total variable costs, and total costs. *Total fixed costs* (TFC) are the costs that the firm incurs in the short run for its fixed inputs; these are constant regardless of the level of output and of whether it produces or not. An example of TFC is the rent that a producer must pay for the factory building over the life of a lease. *Total variable costs* (TVC) are costs incurred by the firm for the variable inputs it uses. These vary directly with the level of output produced and are zero when output is zero. Examples of TVC are raw material costs and some labor costs. *Total costs* (TC) are equal to the sum of total fixed costs and total variable costs.

Though total costs are very important, per-unit or average costs are even more important in the short-run analysis of the firm. The short-run per-unit costs that we consider are the average fixed cost, the average variable cost, the average cost, and the marginal cost. *Average fixed cost* (AFC) equals total fixed costs divided by output. *Average variable cost* (AVC) equals total variable costs divided by output. *Average cost* (AC) equals total costs divided by output; AC also equals AFC plus AVC. Marginal cost (MC) equals the change in TC or the change in TVC per unit change in output.

Example 12.2

Table 12.1 presents the AFC, AVC, AC, and MC schedules derived from the TFC, TVC, and TC schedules. The AFC schedule (column 5) is obtained by dividing TFC (column 2) by the corresponding quantities of output produced (Q in column 1). The AVC schedule (column 6) is obtained by dividing TVC (column 3) by Q. The AC schedule (column 7) is obtained by dividing TC (column 4) by Q. The MC schedule (column 8) is obtained by subtracting successive values of TC (column 4) or TVC (column 3). Thus, MC does not depend on the level of TFC.

Table 12.1

(1) Q	(2) TFC ($)	(3) TVC ($)	(4) TC ($)	(5) AFC ($)	(6) AVC ($)	(7) AC ($)	(8) MC ($)
1	60	30	90	60	30	90	10
2	60	40	100	30	20	50	5
3	60	45	105	20	15	35	10
4	60	55	115	15	13.75	28.75	20
5	60	75	135	12	15	27	45
6	60	120	180	10	20	30	

The AFC, AVC, AC, and MC schedules of Table 12.1 are graphed in Figure 12-1.

Note that the values of the MC schedule (from column 8) are plotted halfway between successive levels of output. Also note that while the AFC curve falls continuously as output is expanded, the AVC, AC, and MC curves are U-shaped. The MC curve reaches its lowest point at a lower level of output than either the AVC curve or the AC curve. Also, the rising portion of the MC curve intersects the AVC and AC curves at their lowest points. This will always be the case.

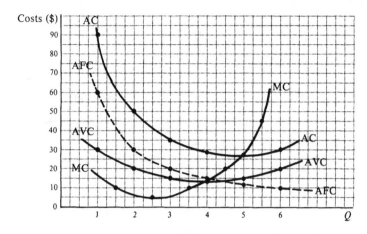

Figure 12-1

⭐ Note!

The law of diminishing returns is the reason that
the marginal cost curve is U-shaped.

Long-Run Costs

In the long run, there are no fixed factors, and a firm can build a plant of
any size. Once a firm has constructed a particular plant, it operates in the
short run. A plant size can be represented by its short-run average cost
(SAC) curve. Larger plants can be represented by SAC curves, which lie
further to the right. The long-run average cost (LAC) curve shows the
minimum per-unit costs of producing each level of output when any de-
sired size of plant can be built. The LAC curve is thus formed from the
relevant segment of the SAC curves.

Example 12.3

Figure 12-2 shows four hypothetical plant sizes that a firm could build in
the long run. Each plant is shown by a SAC curve. To produce up to 300

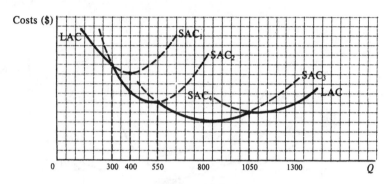

Figure 12-2

units of output, the firm should build and utilize plant 1 (given by SAC_1). From 300 to 550 units of output, it should build the larger plant given by SAC_2, etc. Note that the firm could produce an output of 400 with plant 1, but only at a higher cost than with plant 2. The irrelevant portions of the SAC curves are dashed. The remaining (undashed) portions form the LAC curve. By drawing many more SAC curves, we would get a smoother LAC curve.

If in the long run we increase all factors used in production by a given proportion, there are three possible outcomes: (1) output increases in the same proportion, so that there are constant returns to scale or constant costs; (2) output increases by a greater proportion, giving increasing returns to scale or decreasing costs; and (3) output increases in a smaller proportion, giving decreasing returns to scale or increasing costs. Increasing returns to scale or economies of mass production may result because of division of labor and specialization in production. Beyond a certain size, however, management problems resulting in decreasing returns to scale may arise.

Remember

The LAC curve derives its shape from the possible SAC curves that a firm has over ranges of outputs.

Example 12.4

The LAC curve of Figure 12-2 at first shows increasing returns to scale. Then for a small range of outputs (around 800 units), it shows constant returns to scale. For larger outputs, we have decreasing returns to scale. Whether and when this occurs in the real world depends on the firm and industry under consideration.

True or False Questions

1. Implicit costs are the costs of factors of production owned by the firm.
2. The law of diminishing returns holds in both the short-run and long-run periods.
3. TFC is constant regardless of the level of firm output.
4. TC is zero when the firm does not produce any output.
5. Decreasing costs refers to the situation wherein output increases proportionately more than inputs.

Answers: 1. True; 2. False; 3. True; 4. False; 5. True

Solved Problems

Solved Problem 12.1 A firm pays $200,000 in wages, $50,000 in interest on borrowed money capital, and $70,000 for the yearly rental of its factory building. If the entrepreneur worked for somebody else as a manager she would earn at most $40,000 per year, and if she lent out her money capital to somebody else in a similarly risky business, she would at most receive $10,000 per year. She owns no land or building.

a. Calculate the entrepreneur's economic profit if she received $400,000 from selling her year's output.

b. How much profit is the entrepreneur earning from the point of view of the person on the street? To what is the difference in the results due?

c. What would happen if the entrepreneur's total revenue were $360,000 instead?

Solution:

a. The explicit costs of this entrepreneur are $320,000 ($200,000 in wages plus $50,000 in interest plus $70,000 in rents). Her implicit costs are $50,000 ($40,000 in wages in her best alternative employment plus $10,000 interest on her money capital). Thus, her total costs are $370,000. Since the total revenue from selling the year's output is $400,000, she earns an economic profit of $30,000 for the year.

b. The person on the street would instead say that this entrepreneur's profit is $80,000 (the total revenue of $400,000 minus the out-of-pocket expenditures, or explicit costs, of $320,000). However, $50,000 of this $80,000 represents the normal return on the entrepreneur's owned factors and is appropriately considered a cost by the economist.

c. If the entrepreneur's total revenue were $360,000, she would earn less than a normal return on her owned factors (her wage and interest in alternative employment) and it would be best to eventually go out of business and work as a manager for and lend her money to someone else. This shows that implicit costs are part of the costs of production because they must be covered in order for the firm to remain in business and continue to supply the goods and services it produces.

Solved Problem 12.2

a. Why are the MC, AVC, and AC curves U-shaped?

b. Why does the MC curve intersect the AVC and AC curves at their respective lowest points?

Solution:

a. As we start using variable factors with some fixed factors, we may first obtain increasing returns, but eventually diminishing returns will set in. As a result, the MC, AVC, and AC curves first fall but eventually rise, giving them their U shapes.

b. The MC curve always intersects the AVC and AC curves at their respective lowest points because as long as MC is below AC, it pulls the average down. When the MC is above AC, it pulls the average up. Only when MC equals AC is AC neither falling nor rising (i.e., AC is at its lowest point). This is logical. For example, if your grade on a quiz is lower than your previous average, your average will fall and vice versa.

Chapter 13
PERFECT COMPETITION

IN THIS CHAPTER:

✔ *Perfect Competition Defined*

✔ *Profit Maximization in the Short Run*

✔ *Short-Run Profit or Loss*

✔ *Long-Run Equilibrium*

✔ *True or False Questions*

✔ *Solved Problems*

Perfect Competition Defined

An industry is said to be perfectly competitive if: (1) it is composed of a large number of independent sellers of a commodity, each too small to affect the commodity price; (2) all firms in the industry sell homogenous (identical) products; and (3) there is perfect mobility of resources, so firms can enter or leave the industry in the long run without much difficulty. As a result, the perfectly competitive firm is a "price taker" and can sell any amount of the commodity at the prevailing market price.

   Perhaps the closest we come to perfect competition is in the market for such agricultural commodities as wheat and cotton. There, we may have a large number of producers each too small to affect commodity price. The output of each farmer (say wheat of a given grade) is identical, and it is rather easy to enter or leave this industry. The perfectly competitive model is used to analyze markets, such as these, that approximate perfect competition. It is also used to evaluate the efficiency of the other forms of market organization to be covered in subsequent chapters.

Note!

Perfect competition is rarely seen in the real world, but is an economic benchmark for all types of businesses.

Profit Maximization in the Short Run

A firm maximizes total profits in the short run when the (positive) difference between total revenue (TR) and total costs (TC) is greatest. TR equals price times quantity.

In general, it is more useful to analyze the short-run behavior of the firm by using the marginal-revenue–marginal-cost approach. *Marginal revenue* (MR) is the change in TR per unit change in the quantity sold. Since the perfectly competitive firm can sell any quantity of the commodity at the prevailing price, its $MR = P$, and the demand curve it faces is horizontal at that price. The perfectly competitive firm maximizes its short-run total profits at the output at which MR or P equals MC (and MC is rising).

Example 13.1

In Table 13.1, MR (column 4) is the change in TR and is recorded *between* the various quantities sold. MC (column 7) is the change in TC and is also entered between the various levels of output. Profit per unit (column 10) equals $P - AC$. Total profits (column 11) equal profits per unit times the quantities sold. Note that total profits are maximized at \$16.90 when the firm produces and sells 6.5 units of output where $MR = MC$.

Table 13.1

(1)	(2)	(3)	(4)	(5)	(6)	(7)	(8)	(9)	(10)	(11)
									Profit per	Total
Q	P ($)	TR ($)	MR ($)	TVC ($)	TC ($)	MC ($)	AVC ($)	AC ($)	Unit ($)	Profits ($)
0	8	0		0	8		—	—	—	− 8
1	8	8	8	12	20	12	12	20	−12	−12
2	8	16	8	15	23	3	7.5	11.50	− 3.50	− 7
3	8	24	8	16	24	1	5.33	8	0	0
4	8	32	8	17.40	25.40	1.40	4.35	6.35	+ 1.65	+ 6.60
5	8	40	8	20	28	2.60	4	5.60	+ 2.40	+12
6	8	48⌐	8	24	32⌐	4	4	5.33	+ 2.67	+16.02
*6.5	8	52	8	27.10	35.10	8	4.17	5.40	+ 2.60	+16.90*
7	8	56⌐	8	32	40⌐	24	4.57	5.71	+ 2.29	+16.03
8	8	64		56	64		7	8	0	0

Example 13.2

The profit-maximizing (or best) level of output of this firm can also be viewed in Figure 13-1. The MC and AC values are from Table 13.1. The demand curve facing the firm is horizontal at $P = \$8 = $ MR. As long as MR exceeds MC, it pays for the firm to expand output. Thus, the firm maximizes its total profits at the output level of 6.5 units (given by point C where MR = MC). The profit per unit at this level of output is CF, or $2.60, and total profit is given by the area of rectangle CFGH, which equals $16.90.

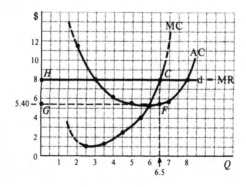

Figure 13-1

Remember

MR = MC is the key to profit maximization.

Short-Run Profit or Loss

If, at the point where $P = MR = MC$, P exceeds AC, the firm is maximizing its total profits. If $P = AC$, the firm is breaking even. If P is larger than AVC but smaller than AC, the firm minimizes total losses. If P is smaller than AVC, the firm minimizes total losses by shutting down. Thus, $P = AVC$ is the shutdown point for the firm.

 **Note!**

A business first determines the profit-maximizing quantity and then determines whether it will have a profit or loss.

Since the perfectly competitive firm always produces where $P = MR = MC$ (as long as P exceeds AVC), the firm's short-run supply curve is given by the rising portion of its MC curve over and above its AVC, or shutdown point.

Long-Run Equilibrium

If the firms in a perfectly competitive industry are making short-run profits, more firms will enter the industry in the long run. This increases market supply of the commodity and reduces the market price until all profits are competed away and all firms just break even. The exact opposite occurs if we start with firms with short-run losses. As a result, all firms in a perfectly competitive industry with long-run equilibrium produce where P = lowest LAC and resources are utilized in the most efficient way.

True or False Questions

1. In a perfectly competitive industry, each firm can affect the commodity price.

2. The marginal revenue of a firm in perfect competition is equal to the commodity price.

3. The perfectly competitive firm maximizes profits at the quantity where its MR curve intersects the rising portion of its MC curve.

4. A firm breaks even when price equals its average variable cost.

5. All firms in perfect competition break even in the long run.

Answers: 1. False; 2. True; 3. True; 4. False; 5. True

Solved Problems

Solved Problem 13.1

a. Define marginal revenue. How is it calculated? Why is marginal revenue constant and equal to price under perfect competition?

b. What is the shape and elasticity of the demand curve facing a perfectly competitive firm? Why?

c. How does the firm determine how much to produce in the short run?

Solution:

a. MR is defined as the change in TR for a one-unit change in the quantity sold. Since the perfectly competitive firm can sell any amount of the commodity at the prevailing market price, its MR is constant. For example, if $P = \$4$, TR $= \$4$ when the firms sells one unit and TR $= \$8$ for two units. Thus, MR = change in TR $= \$4 = P$.

b. Since the perfectly competitive firm can sell any amount at the market price, the demand curve it faces is horizontal or infinitely elastic at this price. With a horizontal demand curve, an infinitely small fall in price causes an infinitely large increase in sales because all consumers will go to the seller with the lowest price. As the denominator of the elasticity formula (the percentage change in price) approaches zero and the numerator (the percentage change in quantity) becomes very large, the value of the fraction and elasticity (E_D) approaches infinity.

c. We can determine how much a firm produces in the short run by making the reasonable assumption that the firm wants to maximize its total profits or minimize its total losses. The general rule is that the firm should expand its output until MR = MC (as long as P exceeds AVC). A firm should expand its output as long as the addition to TR from an additional unit sold (its MR) exceeds the addition to TC to produce this extra unit (its MC). As long as MR > MC, the firm can increase its total profits by expanding output. The firm should not produce any unit for which MR < MC. If it did, it would be adding more to its TC than to its TR and its total profits would fall.

Solved Problem 13.2 From Figure 13-2, set up a table indicating for each alternative demand curve, the best level of output, AC, profit per unit, total profits, whether the firm produces or not, and whether it makes profits or losses (if TFC = $65).

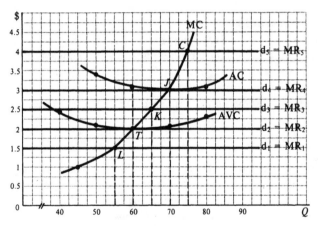

Figure 13-2

Solution: Table 13.2 shows that with d_5, the firm maximizes total profits.

Table 13.2

Demand	Q	AC ($)	Profit per Unit ($)	Total Profits ($)	Result
d_5 ($P = \$4$)	75 (point C)	3.03	0.97	+72.75	Total profits maximized
d_4 ($P = \$3$)	70 (point J)	3	0	0	Break-even point
d_3 ($P = \$2.50$)	65 (point K)	3.02	−0.52	−33.80	Total losses minimized
d_2 ($P = \$2$)	60 (point T)	3.08	−1.08	−64.80	Shutdown point
d_1 ($P = \$1.50$)	55 (point L)	3.18	−1.68	−92.40	Firm does not produce

With d_4, $P = AC$ so that the firm breaks even. With d_3, the firm minimizes total losses at \$33.80 by producing 65 units of output. If the firm stopped producing, it would incur losses equal to its TFC of \$65. Thus, by producing, the firm recovers all of its TVC plus part of TFC. With d_2, the firm's total losses equal \$65 (by rounding) whether it produces or not. This is the shutdown point for the firm. With d_1, the best level of output is 55 units where MR = MC). At this output, the firm's total losses would equal \$92.40. But by stopping production altogether and going out of business, the firm would lose only \$65 (its TFC). Thus, the firm would not produce at $P = \$1.50$.

Solved Problem 13.3 Discuss the advantages of perfect competition.

Solution: The most important advantages of the perfectly competitive form of market organization are that resources are utilized in the most efficient way to produce the goods and services most wanted by society and that consumers pay the lowest possible prices. In long-run equilibrium, each perfectly competitive firm operates the optimum scale of plant at the optimum level of output. This is given by the lowest point of the SAC curve, which generates the lowest point of the LAC curve. Resources could not possibly be arranged more efficiently. Furthermore, since the forces of competition eliminate all profits in the long run, consumers get the good or service at $P =$ lowest LAC. Finally, since the price of the commodity measures the utility of the last unit of the commodity consumed, and this is equated to the MC of producing this unit, there is no better use of these resources. That is, the same resources could not be used to produce goods and services that give greater utility to consumers. Thus, perfect competition is used as the standard against which the efficiency of other market forms is compared.

IN THIS CHAPTER:

✔ *Monopoly Defined*
✔ *Profit Maximization*
✔ *Price Discrimination*
✔ *Regulation of Monopoly*
✔ *True or False Questions*
✔ *Solved Problems*

Monopoly Defined

Pure monopoly is the form of market organization in which there is a single seller of a commodity for which there are no close substitutes. Thus, it is at the opposite extreme from perfect competition. Monopoly may be the result of: (1) increasing returns to scale; (2) control over the supply of raw materials; (3) patents; or (4) government franchise.

For example, electrical companies, telephone companies, and other "public utilities" usually have increasing returns to scale (i.e., falling long-run average costs) over a sufficient range of outputs as to enable a single firm to satisfy the entire market at a lower per-unit cost than two or more firms could. These natural monopolies usually operate under a

government franchise and are subject to government regulation. A monopoly may also arise because a firm may own a patent which precludes other firms from producing the same commodity.

Under pure monopoly, the firm *is* the industry and faces the negatively sloped industry demand curve for the commodity. As a result, if the monopolist wants to sell more of the commodity, it must lower its price. Thus, for a monopolist, MR is less than *P*, and its MR curve lies below its demand curve.

Important!

A monopoly is opposite of perfect competition in every facet of its organization.

Profit Maximization

The profit-maximizing or best level of output for the monopolist is the output at which MR = MC. Price is then read off the demand curve. Depending on the level of AC at this output, the monopolist can have profits, break even, or minimize the short-run total losses.

Example 14.1

From Table 14.1, the monopolist maximizes total profits at $3.75 when it produces and sells 2.5 units of output at the price of $5.50. At this output, MR = MC = $3. As long as MR > MC, the monopolist will expand output and sales because doing so adds more to TR than to TC (and profits

Table 14.1

(1) P ($)	(2) Q	(3) TR ($)	(4) MR ($)	(5) TC ($)	(6) MC ($)	(7) AC ($)	(8) Profit/Unit ($)	(9) Total Profit ($)
8.00	0	0		6		...	...	− 6.00
7.00	1	7.00	7	8	2	8.00	−1.00	− 1.00
6.00	2	12.00	5	9	1	4.50	+1.50	+ 3.00
*5.50	2.5	13.75	3	10	3	4.00	+1.50	+ 3.75*
5.00	3	15.00		12		4.00	+1.00	+ 3.00
4.00	4	16.00	1	20	8	5.00	−1.00	− 4.00
3.00	5	15.00	−1	35	15	7.00	−4.00	−20.00

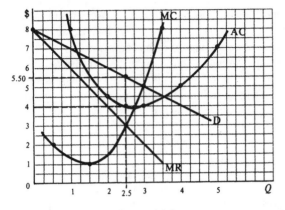

Figure 14-1

rise). The opposite is true when MR < MC. Thus total profits are maximized where MR = MC.

The profit-maximizing or best level of output for this monopolist can also be seen in Figure 14-1 (obtained by plotting the value of columns 1, 2, 4, 6, and 7 of Table 14.1). In this figure, the best level of output is at the point where MR = MC. At this best output level of 2.5 units, the monopolist makes a profit of $1.50 per unit (the vertical distance between D and AC at 2.5 units of output) and $3.75 in total (2.5 units times the $1.50 profit per unit). Note that since P > MR where MR = MC, the rising portion of the MC curve above the AVC does not represent the monopolist supply curve. In the long run, the monopolist can adjust the scale of plant, and profits may persist because of blocked or restricted entry.

 **Note!**

Even though organized completely differently from a perfect competitor, a monopolist still maximizes profit where MR = MC.

Price Discrimination

A monopolist can increase TR and profits at a given level of output and TC by practicing price discrimination. This involves charging different prices for the commodity for different quantities purchased, to different classes of consumers, or in different markets.

For example, a telephone company may charge individuals 15 cents for each of the first 50 telephone calls made during each month, 10 cents for each of the next 100 calls, and so on. Electrical companies usually charge less per kilowatt-hour to industrial users than to households because industrial users have more substitutes available (such as generating their own electricity) and thus have a more elastic demand curve than households.

Regulation of Monopoly

Since a monopoly produces output where MR = MC and $P >$ MR, the monopolist produces less and charges a higher price than a perfect competitor with the same cost curves. For example, if Figure 14-1 was for a perfectly competitive industry, output would be 3 units and price $5 (given where $P =$ MC), rather than $Q = 2.5$ and $P = \$5.50$ for the monopolist. Thus, monopoly leads to a misallocation of resources.

For efficiency considerations, government (federal, state, or local) often allows natural monopolies (such as public utilities) to operate but subjects them to regulation. This usually takes the form of setting a price that allows the monopolist to earn the "normal or fair" return of about 8–10 percent on its investment. However, such regulation only partly corrects the more serious problem of misallocation of resources.

Remember

Monopolies rarely exist in the real world except when regulated by a government body.

True or False Questions

1. Pure monopoly is the opposite of perfect competition.
2. The monopoly maximizes profit at the output level where $P = MC$.
3. The monopolist always earns profits in the short run.
4. A monopoly leads to a higher commodity price and less output than perfect competition.
5. All monopoly profits disappear in the long run.

Answers: 1. True; 2. False; 3. False; 4. True; 5. False

Solved Problems

Solved Problem 14.1

a. Draw a figure showing, for a monopolist, the best level of output. Include three alternative AC curves, showing that the firm (1) makes a profit, (2) breaks even, and (3) incurs a loss.

b. What would happen to this monopolist in the long run if it incurs short-run losses? Short-run profits?

Solution:

a. In Figure 14-2, the best level of output for the monopolist is OB, given by point C where $MR = MC$. With AC_1, the monopolist makes a per-unit profit of GF and a total profit of GF times OB. With AC_2, $P = AC$ and the monopolist breaks even. With AC_3, the monopolist incurs a per-unit loss of HG and a total loss of HG times OB. Only if $P > AVC$ (so that $TR > TVC$) will the monopolist stay in business and minimize short-run total losses by producing OB.

b. If the monopolist has short-run losses, it could, in the long run, build a more appropriate scale of plant to produce the best long-run level of output. The monopolist might also advertise in an attempt to cause an upward shift in the demand curve it faces. (This, however, will also shift cost curves up.) If this monopolist still incurs a loss after having considered all of these possibilities, it will stop producing the commodity in the long run. If the monopolist was already making short-run profits, it will still build the most appropriate plant in the long run and increase total profits.

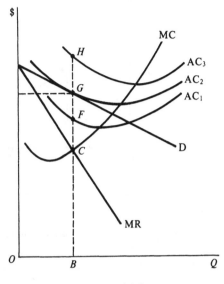

Figure 14-2

Solved Problem 14.2 Refer to Figure 14-3, which contains the market demand curve facing a monopolist.

a. What price should the monopolist charge without price discrimination if its best level of output (given by the point where MR = MC) is *OB*? What would the TR be? How much is the consumers' surplus?

b. Suppose the monopolist sold *OA* units at price *OF*. In order to induce consumers to buy *AB* additional units, it lowers its price to *OC* only on *AB* units. How much would TR be now? How much of the consumers' surplus remains?

Solution:

a. The highest price the monopolist can charge (without price discrimination) to sell *OB* units is *OC*. The TR would then equal the area of rectangle *OCKB*. Consumers' surplus is *CGK*.

b. TR is *OFHA* (for *OA* units) plus *AJKB* (for *AB* units). Note that price discrimination has increased TR by *CFHJ* (and this is the amount by which the consumers' surplus declined). Consumers' surplus is now only *FGH* plus *HKJ*.

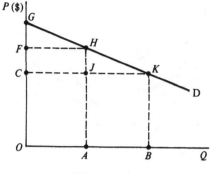

Figure 14-3

Solved Problem 14.3

a. Should the government break up a monopoly into a large number of perfectly competitive firms? Why?

b. Does monopoly lead to more technological progress than perfect competition? Why?

Solution:

a. In industries operating under cost conditions (such as constant returns to scale) that make the existence of perfect competition feasible, the dissolution of a monopoly (by government antitrust action) into a large number of perfectly competitive firms will result in a greater long-run equilibrium output for the industry, a lower commodity price, and usually a lower LAC than under monopoly. However, because of cost and technological conditions, it is not desirable to break up a natural monopoly into a large number of perfectly competitive firms. In dealing with natural monopolies, the government usually chooses to regulate them rather than break them up.

b. There is a great deal of disagreement on whether monopoly or perfect competition leads to more technological progress. Since a monopolist usually makes long-run profits while perfect competitors do not, the monopolist has more resources to devote to research and development (R & D). The monopolist is also more likely to retain the benefits of the technological advance it introduces. A technological advance introduced by a perfect competitor which leads to lower costs and short-run profits is easily and quickly copied by other firms, and this eliminates the profits of the firm that introduced it. On the other hand, a monopolist may feel very secure in its position and have no incentive to engage in research and development and to innovate.

Chapter 15
MONOPOLISTIC COMPETITION AND OLIGOPOLY

IN THIS CHAPTER:

✔ *Monopolistic Competition Defined*
✔ *Profit Maximization*
✔ *Oligopoly Defined*
✔ *Collusion*
✔ *Long-Run Efficiency Implications*
✔ *True or False Questions*
✔ *Solved Problems*

Monopolistic Competition Defined

In *monopolistic competition* there are many firms selling a differentiated product or service. It is a blend of competition and monopoly. The competitive elements result from the large number of firms and the easy entry. The monopoly element results from differentiated (i.e., similar but not identical) products or services. Product differentiation may be real or imaginary and can be created through advertising. However, the availability of close substitutes severely limits the "monopoly" power of each firm.

Monopolistic competition is the most prevalent form of market organization in retailing. The numerous grocery stores, gasoline stations, dry cleaners, etc. within close proximity of each other are good examples. Examples of differentiated products include the numerous brands of headache remedies (e.g., aspirin, Bufferin, Excedrin, etc.), soaps, detergents, breakfast cereals, and cigarettes. Even if the differences are imaginary (as in the case of various brands of aspirin), they are economically important if the consumer is willing to pay a little more or travel a little further for a preferred brand.

You Need to Know ✔

Most businesses fit under the category of monopolistic competition in terms of market organization.

Profit Maximization

The monopolistic competitor faces a demand curve which is negatively sloped (because of product differentiation) but highly elastic (because of the availability of close substitutes). The monopolistic competitor's profit-maximizing or best level of output is the output at which MR = MC, provided $P > $ AVC. At that output, the firm can make a profit, break even, or minimize losses in the short run. In the long run, firms are either attracted into an industry by short-run profits or leave it if faced with losses until the demand curve (d) facing remaining firms is tangent to its AC curve, and the firm breaks even ($P = $ AC).

Example 15.1

Panel A of Figure 15-1 shows a monopolistic competitor producing 550 units of output (where MR = MC), selling it at $10.50 (on d), and making a profit of $3.50 per unit and $1925 in total. These profits attract more firms into the industry. This causes a downward (leftward) shift in this firm's demand curve to d′ (in Panel B), at which the firm sells 400 units at $8 and breaks even. Since $P > $ MR where MR = MC, the MC curve above AVC does not represent the firm's supply curve.

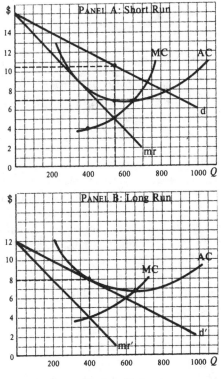

Figure 15-1

Oligopoly Defined

Oligopoly is the form of market organization in which there are few sellers of a product. If the product is homogenous, there is a pure oligopoly. If the product is differentiated, there is a differentiated oligopoly. Since there are only a few sellers of a product, the actions of each seller affect others. That is, the firms are mutually interdependent.

★ Note!

It is difficult to graphically analyze an oligopoly (as we do with the other types of market organizations) due to the mutual interdependence among the firms.

Pure oligopoly is found in the production of cement, aluminum, and many other industrial products which are are virtually standardized. Examples of differentiated oligopolies are industries producing automobiles, cigarettes, PCs, and most electrical appliances, where three or four large firms dominate the market. Because of mutual interdependence, if one firm lowered its price, it could take most of the sales away from the other firms. Other firms are then likely to retaliate and possibly start a price war. As a result, there is a strong compulsion for oligopolists not to change prices but, rather, to compete on the basis of quality, product design, customer service, and advertising.

Collusion

An orderly price change (i.e., one that does not start a price war) is usually accomplished by collusion that can be overt or tacit. The most extreme form of overt collusion is the centralized cartel, in which the oligopolists produce the monopoly output, charge the monopoly price, and somehow allocate production and profits among the cartel members. Antitrust laws make overt collusion illegal in the U.S. In tacit collusion, the oligopolists informally follow a recognized price leader in their pricing policies or agree on how to share the market.

Until the 1980s, U.S. Steel (now called USX) was a recognized price leader. When rising costs required it, U.S. Steel raised the price on some of its products on the tacit understanding that other domestic steel producers would match the price within a few days. An orderly price increase was thus achieved without exposing producers to government antitrust action or the danger of a price war.

Long-Run Efficiency Implications

The monopolistically competitive firm misallocates resources because it produces where $P > MC$ (see Figure 15-1). In addition, it does not produce at the lowest point on its LAC curve as a perfect competitor does. However, these inefficiencies are usually not great because of the highly elastic demand faced by monopolistic competitors.

In contrast to the perfect competitor, the monopolistic competitor engages in nonprice competition, which takes the form of advertising and product differentiation. Such tactics are intended to increase the firm's share of the market and shift its demand curve upward (to the right). However, they also increase the firm's costs and shift the firm's cost curves upward. While some advertising informs the consumer and product differentiation satisfies the consumers' desire for variety, both may be excessive and wasteful.

While the oligopolist can make profits, break even, or incur losses in the short run, in the long run the firm will leave the industry rather than incur losses. Oligopolists underallocate resources and can earn long-run profits because of restricted entry. Usually they also engage in excessive advertising and product differentiation. However, efficiency considerations may allow only a few firms in the industry, and oligopolists may use their profits for research and development.

Don't Forget!

Monopolistic competitors and oligopolists are like monopolists in that they do not allocate resources as efficiently as perfect competitors, as far as society is concerned.

True or False Questions

1. The monopoly power of a monopolistic competitor is limited by the availability of close substitutes.

2. A monopolistic competitor produces at the lowest point on its LAC curve.

3. Restricted entry is a characteristic of monopolistic competition.

4. In tacit collusion, oligopolists meet and decide on a price leader to follow in their pricing policies.

5. In the long run oligopolists can earn profits.

Answers: 1. True; 2. False; 3. False; 4. False; 5. True

Solved Problems

Solved Problem 15.1

a. Why does a prospective monopolistic competitor find it relatively easy to start production in the long run?

b. Why does the demand curve of a monopolistic competitor shift down when more firms start production?

c. Why is it difficult or impossible to define the industry under monopolistic competition?

d. Why is there a cluster of prices rather than a single equilibrium price in this kind of industry?

Solution:

a. A prospective monopolistic competitor usually finds it relatively easy to start production because very little capital and no great technical know-how are required to open a small gasoline station, grocery store, barber shop, etc.

b. When more firms start producing a differentiated product, the demand curve of previously existing monopolistic competitors shifts down because each firm now has a smaller share of the market.

c. Technically speaking, we cannot define the monopolistically competitive industry because each firm produces a somewhat different product. We simply cannot add together aspirins, Bufferins, Excedrins, etc. to get the market demand and supply curve because they are similar, but not identical, products. Thus, our graphical analysis must be confined to the "typical" or "representative" firm.

d. Slightly differentiated products also permit and cause slightly different prices. That is, even in long-run equilibrium, there will be a cluster of equilibrium prices, one for each differentiated product, rather than a single, industry-wide equilibrium price.

Solved Problem 15.2

a. What are some of the natural and artificial barriers to entry into oligopolistic industries?

b. What are the possible harmful effects of oligopoly?

c. What are the possible beneficial effects of oligopoly?

Solution:

a. The natural barriers to entry into oligopolistic industries like the automobile, aluminum, and steel industries are the smallness of the markets in relation to efficient operation and the huge amounts of capital and specialized inputs required to start efficient operation. Some artificial barriers to entry are control over raw materials, patents, and government franchise. When entry is blocked or at least restricted, the firms in an oligopolistic industry can earn long-run profits.

b. In the long run, oligopoly may lead to the following harmful effects: (1) $P > MC$ and so there is an underallocation of the economy's resources to the firms in the oligopolistic industry; (2) the oligopolist usually does not produce at the lowest point on its LAC curve; and (3) when oligopolists produce a differentiated product, too much may be spent on advertising and model changes.

c. For technological reasons, many products (such as automobiles, steel, etc.) cannot be produced under conditions of perfect competition (because their cost of production would be prohibitively high). In addition, oligopolists spend a great deal of their profits on research and development, and this may lead to faster technological advance and a higher standard of living than if the industry were organized along more competitive lines. Finally, some advertising is useful since it informs customers, and some product differentiation has the economic value of satisfying the different tastes of different consumers.

Chapter 16

DEMAND FOR ECONOMIC RESOURCES

IN THIS CHAPTER:

✔ *Resource Pricing*
✔ *Resource Demand*
✔ *Changes in Resource Demand*
✔ *True or False Questions*
✔ *Solved Problems*

Resource Pricing

We now examine how the prices of productive resources such as wages, rents, interest, and profits are determined in a mixed economy. Resource prices are a major determinant of money incomes and of the allocation of resources to various uses and firms.

Broadly speaking, the price of a resource is determined by its market demand and supply. Firms demand resources in order to produce commodities. The demand for resources is a derived demand—derived from the demand for the commodities that require the resources in production. The greater the demand for the commodity and the more productive the resource, the greater the price that firms are willing to pay for the resource.

For example, as a result of consumers' demand for a final commodity, say, shoes, firms hire labor and other resources in order to produce shoes. The greater the demand for shoes, the greater the firms' demands for labor. In the absence of market imperfections (minimum wage laws, union power, etc.), the wage rate of labor is determined exclusively by the market demand and supply of labor.

To derive a firm's demand for a resource, we must first define the marginal revenue product (MRP). MRP measures the increase in the firm's total revenue from selling the extra product that results from employing one additional unit of the resource. If the firm is a perfect competitor in the commodity market, it can sell this extra output at the given market price for the commodity. However, as additional units of the variable resource are used together with fixed resources, after a point the extra output or marginal physical product (MPP) declines because of the operation of the law of diminishing returns. Because of the declining MPP, MRP also declines.

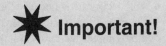 **Important!**

Resources are priced just as goods and services are—by the strength of the demand and supply for them—but resource demand is a derived demand.

Resource Demand

In order to maximize total profits, a firm should hire additional units of a resource as long as each adds more to the firm's total revenue than to its total costs. The increase in total revenue is the MRP. The increase in total cost gives the marginal resource cost (MRC). If the firm is a perfect competitor in the resource market, it can hire any quantity of the variable resource at the given resource price, so MRC equals the resource price. Thus to maximize total profits, the firm should hire the resource until MRP equals the resource price. The declining MRP schedule then represents the firm's demand schedule for the resource.

If the firm is an imperfect competitor in the commodity market, the MRP declines both because the MPP declines and because the firm must lower the commodity price in order to sell more units. If the firm remains a perfect competitor in the resource market, the firm again maximizes total profits when it hires the resource until MRP equals the resource price. The declining MRP schedule then represents the firm's demand schedule for the variable resource.

Example 16.1

In Table 16.1, column 1 refers to units of a variable resource, say, labor, employed in a given plant. Column 2 gives the total product produced. Column 3 gives the marginal physical product or the change in total product per unit change in the use of the resource. Commodity price (column 4) declines because of imperfect competition in the commodity market. TR (column 5) is obtained by multiplying commodity price by total product. Column 6 gives the MRP, measured as the change in total revenue. MRP declines both because MPP declines and because the product price declines. A firm that is a perfect competitor in the resource market would maximize its total profits by employing the resource until the MRP equals the resource price.

Table 16.1

(1) Units of Resource	(2) Total Product	(3) MPP or Δ (2)	(4) Product Price	(5) Total Revenue (2) × (4)	(6) MRP or Δ (5)
0	0		$11	$ 0	
1	5	5	10	50	50
2	9	4	9	81	31
3	12	3	8	96	15
4	14	2	7	98	2
5	15	1	6	90	-8

The declining MRP schedule of columns 6 and 1 in Table 16.1 is the firm's demand schedule for the resource and is graphed as d' in Figure 16-1. At the resource price of $50, the firm will hire one unit of the resource. At the resource price of $31, the firm will hire two units of the resource, and so on.

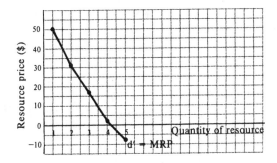

Figure 16-1

Changes in Resource Demand

A firm's demand for a productive resource will increase (i.e., shift up) if:
(1) the product demand increases; (2) the productivity of the resource rises; (3) the prices of substitute resources rise; or (4) the prices of complementary resources fall.

Remember

A firm's demand for a resource (say, labor) depends in large part upon circumstances beyond the firm's control.

For example, if the market demand for shoes rises and if the firm provides each worker with better but more expensive equipment, the firm's demand for labor will also rise. That is, to produce more shoes requires more labor; better equipment makes labor more productive so the demand for labor increases; an increase in the price of equipment encourages the substitution of labor for capital in production.

If a firm uses more than one variable resource, say labor (L) and capital (K), the firm will maximize total profits when it uses labor and capital until the marginal revenue product of each resource equals the resource price (if the firm is a perfect competitor in the resource markets). That is, the firm will maximize total profits when $MRP_L = P_L$ or wage rate, and $MRP_K = P_K$ or the rate of interest. This can be rewritten as $MRP_L/P_L = MRP_K/P_K = 1$ and can be generalized to any number of resources. If the firm is an imperfect competitor in the resource markets, the profit maximization condition is generalized to $MPP_L = MRC_L$ and $MPP_K = MRC_K$ or $MPP_L/MRC_L = MPP_K/MRC_K = 1$ (where MRC refers to the marginal resource cost).

True or False Questions

1. The price of a resource is determined by the demand for the resource.

2. If the firm is a perfect competitor in the product market, its MRP curve is downward-sloping only because the marginal physical product curve of the resource is downward sloping.

3. Marginal resource cost refers to the increase in the firm's total costs in hiring each additional unit of the resource.

4. To maximize profits, a firm should hire resources as long as each additional unit of the resource adds more to the firm's total costs than to its total revenue.

5. A firm's demand for a resource shifts up if the productivity of the resource increases.

Answers: 1. False; 2. True; 3. True; 4. False; 5. True

Solved Problems

Solved Problem 16.1

a. Why do firms demand resources? In what way is a firm's demand for a resource a derived demand? How does this differ from consumers' demand for final commodities?

b. What determines the strength of a firm's demand for a productive resource?

Solution:

a. Firms demand resources in order to produce final commodities. It is the consumers' demand for final commodities that ultimately gives rise to the firm's demand for productive resources. Because of this, the demand for a resource is referred to as a derived demand. It is derived from the demand for the final commodities that require the resource in production. While consumers demand final commodities because of the direct utility that they get from consuming commodities, producers demand resources only because the resource can be used to produce the commodities that consumers demand.

b. The strength of a firm's demand for a resource depends on: (1) the strength of the demand for the commodity that the resource is used to produce; (2) the productivity of the resource in producing the final commodity; and (3) the prices of other related (i.e., substitute and complementary) resources. The higher the demand for the final commodity, the more productive is the resource. The higher the price of substitute resources and the lower the price of complementary resources, the greater the firm's demand for the resource.

Solved Problem 16.2 From Table 16.2,

a. Find the marginal physical product (MPP), total revenue, and the marginal revenue product (MRP) schedules.

b. Why does the MPP decline? Why does MRP decline? How do we know this firm is a perfect competitor in the product market?

Table 16.2

Units of Resource	Total Product	Product Price
0	0	
1	10	$1
2	18	1
3	24	1
4	28	1
5	30	1

Solution:

a. Column 3 in Table 16.3 gives the MPP. It is obtained from the change in total product per unit change in the use of the variable resource. Column 5 gives the total revenue of the firm. It is obtained by multiplying the product price (column 4) by the total product (column 2). Column

Table 16.3

(1) Units of Resource	(2) Total Product	(3) MPP or Δ(2)	(4) Product Price	(5) Total Revenue (2) × (4)	(6) MRP or Δ (5)
0	0			$ 0	
1	10	10	$1	10	$10
2	18	8	1	18	8
3	24	6	1	24	6
4	28	4	1	28	4
5	30	2	1	30	2

6 gives the marginal revenue product. It is obtained from the increase in the total revenue in column 5.

b. The MPP that results from employing each additional unit of the variable resource (together with fixed amounts of other resources) declines because of the law of diminishing returns. The MRP declines because MPP declines. We know that this firm is a perfect competitor in the product market because product price remains constant at $1 per unit regardless of the quantity of the product sold by the firm.

Solved Problem 16.3 Explain how much of each variable resource a firm should hire in order to maximize total profits, if the firm is an imperfect competitor in the resource markets.

Solution: When an imperfect competitor in the resource markets wants to hire more of a resource, it will have to pay a higher price, not only on the additional units of the resource but also on all previous units of the resource hired. Thus, the increase in the total costs of hiring an additional unit of the resource or marginal resource cost (MRC) exceeds the resource price. The firm will maximize total profits when it hires variable resources as long as each resource MRP exceeds its MRC and until they are equal. With variable resources labor (L) and capital (K), the firm maximizes total profits when $MRP_L = MRC_L$ and $MRP_K = MRC_K$. Another way of stating the profit-maximizing condition is to say that a firm should hire resources until the MRP per dollar spent on each resource is the same. Once again, this rule can be extended to any number of variable resources.

Chapter 17

PRICING OF WAGES, RENT, INTEREST, AND PROFITS

IN THIS CHAPTER:

Wage Determination

The *wage rate* refers to the earnings per hour of labor. The wage rate divided by the price index gives the *real wage rate* or "purchasing power" of wages. We are primarily concerned with real wages.

The level of real wages depends on the productivity of labor. Real wages are higher the greater the amount of capital available per worker, the more advanced the technology, and the greater the availability of natural resources (fertile land, mineral deposits, etc.).

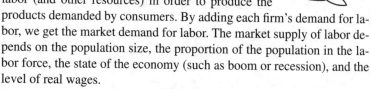

In preceding chapters, we saw that firms demand labor (and other resources) in order to produce the products demanded by consumers. By adding each firm's demand for labor, we get the market demand for labor. The market supply of labor depends on the population size, the proportion of the population in the labor force, the state of the economy (such as boom or recession), and the level of real wages.

The *competitive equilibrium real-wage rate* is determined at the intersection of the market demand and supply of labor curves. The firm then hires labor until the marginal revenue product of labor (MRP_L) or its demand for labor (d_L) equals the wage rate.

Example 17.1

In Panel B of Figure 17-1, the competitive equilibrium real-wage rate of $6 per hour is determined at the intersection of the market demand and supply of labor. The supply of labor to the competitive firm of Panel A (s_L) is horizontal at the wage rate of $6. This means that the firm is so small (say, one of 1,000 identical firms in the market) that it can hire any quantity of labor at the equilibrium market wage rate without affecting that wage rate. To maximize total profits the firm hires 30 units of labor because $MRP_L = W = \$6$ at 30 units of labor.

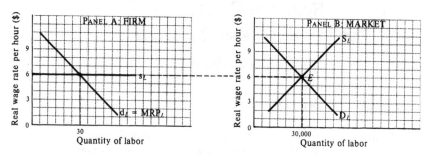

Figure 17-1

Note!

Wages are determined by the intersection of the demand and supply of labor, not just by firms or just by workers.

Workers may not be hired competitively. A dominant employer has monopoly power in the local labor market and is referred to as a monopsonist. It faces the rising market supply curve of labor which indicates that it must pay higher wages to hire more workers. Thus, the change in the total cost of hiring an additional worker or marginal resource cost of labor (MRC_L) exceeds the wage rate. To maximize profits, the firm hires labor until $MRP_L = MRC_L$ and pays the wage indicated on the supply curve of labor for that quantity of labor.

Unions and Wage Differentials

Labor unions attempt to increase wages in three ways. First, unions attempt to increase the demand for labor by increasing productivity, by advertising union-made products, and by lobbying to restrict imports. These are the most desirable but also the least effective methods. Second, unions attempt to raise wages by restricting the supply of labor through the imposition of high initiation fees and long apprenticeships and requirements that employers hire only union members. This is done primarily by craft unions (i.e., unions of such skilled workers as electricians). Third, unions attempt to raise wage rates directly by bargaining with employers, under the threat of a strike. This is the most common method and is used primarily by industrial unions (i.e., unions of all the workers of a particular industry, such as automobile workers). Empirical studies seem to indicate that, in general, unions in the U.S. have raised real wages for their members by only about 10 to 15 percent.

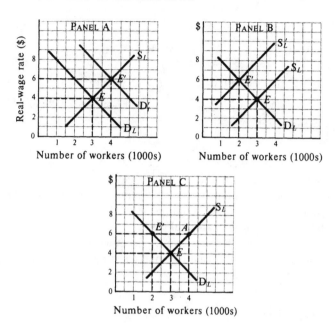

Figure 17-2

Example 17.2

In Panel A of Figure 17-2, the equilibrium real wage rate is $4 and employment is 3000 workers (at point E, where D_L intersects S_L).

If the union can increase D_L to D'_L, $W = \$6$ and employment rises to 4000. Starting from the same original equilibrium point E in Panel B, a craft union could instead attempt to reduce S_L to S'_L so that $W = \$6$ but only 2000 are employed. In Panel C, an industrial union could attempt to negotiate $W = \$6$ at which 2000 workers are employed and another 2000 workers ($E'A$) are unable to find jobs.

If all jobs and individuals were exactly alike and all markets perfectly competitive, there would be a single wage for all jobs and all workers. However, jobs requiring equal qualifications may differ in attractiveness, and higher wages must be paid to attract and retain workers in more unpleasant jobs. Such wage differentials are known as equalizing differences. Even if all jobs were equally attractive, wage differences would persist because individuals such as doctors and clerks differ widely in capacities, skills, training, and education. Thus, labor falls into many non-competing groups, each requiring different training and receiving different wages. Finally, some wage differences are the result of imperfect markets. Market imperfections include lack of information, unwillingness to move, union power, minimum-wage laws, and monopsony power. The wide wage differences actually observed in the real world among different categories of people and jobs are in general the result of a combination of these three factors.

Rent

Rent is the price for the use of land and other natural resources that are fixed in total supply. If all land is alike and has one competitive use (say, the growing of wheat), then rent is determined at the intersection of the market demand curve and the vertical market supply curve of land. Regardless of the market demand and the rent paid, the same amount of land remains available.

You Need to Know ✔

Pricing rent for land is different from pricing other resources in that land is relatively fixed in supply.

Example 17.3

With the supply of land fixed (S) in Figure 17-3, rent is equal to r when the market demand curve for land is D, and r' when it is D'. If from the equilibrium rent of r', the government imposed a tax of $r'r$ on rental incomes, land users would continue to pay r' but landowners would retain only r. The quantity of land supplied, however, would remain unchanged. In the real world, we have different types and uses of land with different rental values. The supply of land can also be increased somewhat (say, by drainage) or reduced (by improper use).

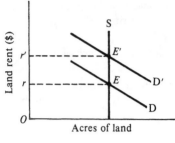

Figure 17-3

Interest

Interest is the price paid for using money or loanable funds, expressed as a percentage of the amount borrowed. If the rate of interest is 8 percent per year, this means that for $100 borrowed today, $108 will have to be repaid a year from today. For simplicity, we discuss the pure rate of interest or the interest on a riskless loan (as on a U.S. government bond). Other interest rates are higher depending on the risk, maturity, administrative cost, and competitiveness of the loanable-funds market.

The equilibrium interest rate is determined at the intersection of the market demand and supply curves of loanable funds. The demand for loanable funds comes from the borrowing of firms, consumers, and government, and is negatively sloped. To maximize profits, a firm will borrow in order to invest in machinery, inventory, etc., as long as the return, or marginal productivity, of the investment exceeds the rate of interest on borrowed funds. Thus, interest rates allocate the scarce loanable funds to the most productive uses. The supply of loanable funds stems from the past and current savings of individuals and firms. It is upward sloped and is greatly affected by monetary policy.

Profits

Economic *profits* are the excess of total revenue over total costs, including both explicit and implicit costs. Profits stem from the introduction of a successful innovation, a reward for uninsurable risk-bearing or uncertainty, and monopoly power. They serve as incentives for innovation, to shift resources to the production of those commodities that society wants most, and as a reward for efficiency.

Firms introduce new products and new production methods in the expectation of profits. If successful, other firms may imitate the successful innovator and compete these profits away. Similarly, more risky ventures (such as petroleum exploration) require the expectation of a higher profit to induce investments. Finally, monopoly power allows a firm to restrict output artificially, keep competitors out, and charge a price that allows profits to persist.

Remember

The search for profits is what brings most new goods and services to the market.

In 1990, the breakdown of U.S. national income was as follows: wages and salaries, 74 percent; proprietors' income, 7 percent, corporate profits, 8 percent; interest, 10 percent; and rents, 1 percent. Since 1990, wages and salaries have increased relatively and proprietors' incomes have fallen relatively. This is due to the increase in the importance of corporations relative to individual-owned businesses.

Epilogue on Commodity and Resource Pricing

In a free-enterprise economy, commodity and factor prices are determined by their respective demands and supplies. Firms demand resources owned by households in order to produce the goods and services demanded by households. Households then use the income they receive to purchase the goods and services produced by firms. This circular flow of economic activity determines what, how, and for whom to produce. It is a general equilibrium system because a change in any part of the economy affects every other part of the economy. When markets are perfectly competitive and are in long-run equilibrium, resources are allocated most efficiently and the economy's output of goods and services is maximized.

In the real world, however, this most efficient resource allocation is difficult to achieve.

True or False Questions

1. The competitive equilibrium real-wage rate is determined at the intersection of the market demand and supply curves of labor.

2. The wage differentials observed in the real world are generally due to market imperfections.

3. The supply curve of land and natural resources is upward-sloping.

4. The factors affecting interest rates are risk, maturity, administrative costs, and competitiveness of the loanable funds market.

5. In order for firms to invest in higher risk ventures the expected profit must be higher.

Answers: 1. True; 2. False; 3. False; 4. True; 5. True

Solved Problems

Solved Problem 17.1

a. On what does the market supply of labor depend?

b. How does the state of the economy affect the market supply of labor?

c. What is the effect of the real-wage rate level on the quantity of labor supplied in the market?

Solution:

a. The market supply of labor depends on the population size, the proportion of the population in the labor force, and the state of the economy. In general, the larger the population and the greater the participation rate of the population in the labor force, the greater the market supply of labor.

b. The state of the economy (boom or recession) affects the market supply of labor. When the economy is booming, many people not previously employed may, attracted by the availability of high-paying jobs, decide to enter the labor force. On the other hand, someone who felt the need to look for a job under less prosperous conditions may leave the labor force when a spouse or parent gets a high-paying job in a booming economy. Thus, the supply of labor may increase, decrease, or remain unchanged depending on the net effect of these two opposing forces. The opposite is true in a recession.

c. The level of real wages also gives rise to two opposing forces affecting the quantity of labor supplied. On the one hand, a high level of real wages induces workers to substitute work for leisure and work more hours per week to take advantage of the high real wages. On the other hand, a high real wage (and income) results in workers demanding more of every normal commodity, including leisure, and working fewer hours per week. Once again, the quantity of labor supplied may increase, decrease, or remain unchanged, depending on the net effect of these two opposing forces.

Solved Problem 17.2 Getting an education and training is sometimes referred to as an "investment in human capital."

a. In what ways is this similar to any other investment?

b. Why is treating education and training as investment in human capital useful?

c. What are its shortcomings?

Solution:

a. Getting an education and training can be considered an investment in human capital because, as with any other investment, it involves a cost and entails a return. The cost of getting an education and training involves such explicit expenses as tuition, books, etc. and such implicit cost as the forgone wages while in school or the lower wages received while in training. The return on education and training takes the form of the higher wages received over the individual's working life. By discounting all costs and extra income to the present and comparing returns to costs, we can calculate the rate of return on the investment in human capital and compare it to the returns from other investments.

b. Viewing education and training as investment in human capital can explain real-world occurrences such as why we educate and train the young more than the old, why young people migrate more readily than old, etc. The answer is that young people have a longer working time over which to receive the benefits of education, training, and migration.

c. Some shortcomings of this line of thinking are as follows: (1) Not all expenses for education and training represent costs. Some should be regarded as consumption since they do not contribute to subsequent higher earnings (for example, when an engineering student takes a course in poetry). (2) Higher subsequent earnings may be the result of innate ability and greater intelligence and effort rather than training.

Solved Problem 17.3

    a. What are the functions of profits?

    b. What are some objections to profits?

Solution:

    a. Profits serve as incentives for innovators to shift resources to the production of those commodities that society wants most, and as a reward for efficiency. The introduction of an innovation involves uncertainty and may result in financial loss if it is not successful. The expectation of a financial reward in the form of profits is required to induce innovations. Similarly, profit in some industries and losses in others is the indication that society wants more commodities from the former and less from the latter. Related to this is the fact that more efficient firms in a given industry are rewarded with profits which they can then use to expand, while less efficient firms incur losses and have to contract operations or go out of business.

    b. Among the objections to profits are the following: (1) Profits arising from monopoly serve no socially useful purpose (except when they lead to more innovations). Therefore, such profits should be taxed away or the monopoly should be regulated (if it is not feasible to break it up). (2) Profits may lead to an excessively unequal distribution of income. This, too, can be corrected by progressive taxation. However, a general attack on all profits is not justified, because profits, as we have seen before, do perform socially useful functions.

Index